# The District Line

M A C Horne FCILT

**Capital Transport**

First published 2006

ISBN 185414 292 5

Published in association with London's Transport Museum
by Capital Transport Publishing, PO Box 250, Harrow, Middlesex

Printed by CS Graphics, Singapore

© M A C Horne 2006

The cover painting is by Peter Green, GRA
The maps are by Mike Harris

## CONTENTS

- 5 ORIGINS AND OPENING
- 12 EXPANSION
- 24 A CIRCLE COMPLETED
- 36 ELECTRIFICATION
- 47 THE DISTRICT IN ITS HEYDAY
- 65 THE LONDON PASSENGER TRANSPORT BOARD
- 78 A NEW ERA
- 93 RECENT TIMES

View taken at the east end of the first station at Earl's Court. The arrival of the station spawned the new housing (in Hogarth Road) seen under construction in the background. In this picture is a very rare view of a District Railway policeman. LT Museum

# Origins and Opening

London Underground's District Line has a long and intricate history. It was not the first Underground railway in London: that honour fell to the Metropolitan Railway (the 'Met'), which opened in 1863. This ran between Farringdon Street and Paddington via King's Cross and was at first operated by the Great Western Railway (GWR). The Met and the underground lines which followed it were responses to the congested state of the road network at ground level, the need for faster communication to, from and within the City, and the need for effective communication between the main line railway termini. By building underground it was possible to avoid the ugly brick viaducts that destroyed homes and devalued property, and which had alienated public opinion. The technical and commercial success of the Met soon spawned ideas for further underground railways, but the problems with smoke in the tunnels and stations was an issue and later lines tended to have more open-air cuttings to reduce the problem.

The Met's engineer, John Fowler, was adroit at recognising new rail opportunities and was alive to the railway potential of the new Westminster–Blackfriars Thames Embankment, authorised in 1862 and upon which work had not yet started. By 1863 he was advocating a railway from Farringdon via the Embankment, Kensington and Notting Hill to meet the Met at Paddington Praed Street, thus transforming the Metropolitan into a 'circular' railway, an idea that soon gained popular appeal.

The Met's success caused an influx of railway schemes applying for Parliamentary powers and caused the House of Lords to establish a committee to identify the best schemes to serve London. The idea of a circular line appealed and when the committee finally reported in July 1863, one of the 18 recommendations was for an 'inner circuit of railway that should abut, if not actually join, nearly all the principal railway termini in the Metropolis'. The committee also felt an equivalent outer circle would be beneficial, connecting London's radial railways and connecting with the inner circle, promoting extensive inter-running. However the schemes that emerged for the 1863–4 Parliamentary session were of widely varying degrees of compliance with the objectives; there was also much overlap and the approval of some schemes would frustrate others, so Parliament was left to extract something workable.

The most compliant scheme was submitted by the promoters of a 'Metropolitan District Railway' which envisaged an outer circle commencing by a junction with the London, Chatham & Dover Railway at Wandsworth Road and proceeding via Clapham Junction, Kensington High Street then Kilburn in the north, Rotherhithe in the east, thence via the London, Brighton & South Coast's South London line from which trains could get back to Wandsworth Road. Near what is now Earl's Court a branch would run west to divide near Warwick Road into north and south facing connections with the West London Railway (WLR) or West London Extension Railway (WLER) while another branch would link to an inner circle, running via the new Thames embankment to Tower Hill. The inner circle would be completed by the Met which formed the north side of the circle and would build extensions at the eastern and western ends to meet the newcomer.

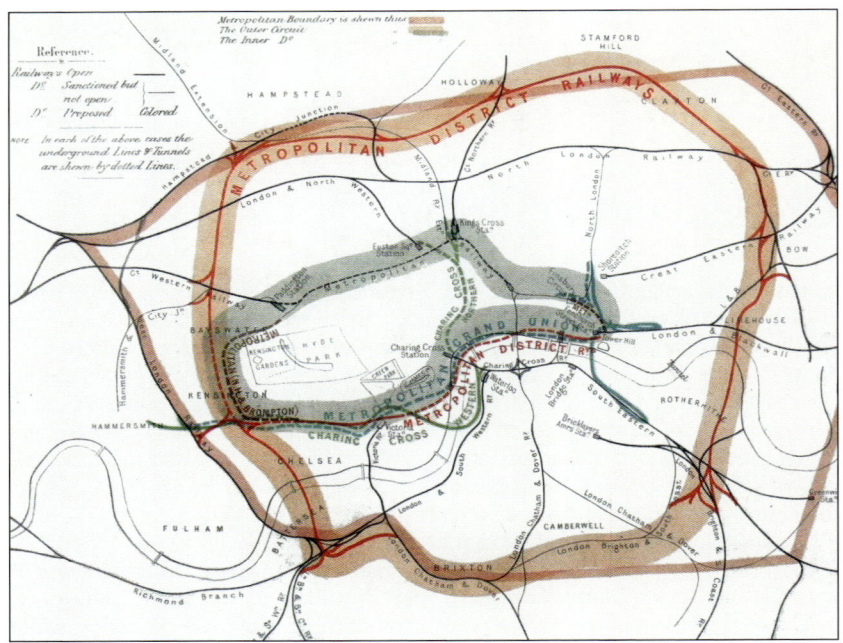

Map of the underground railways proposed in 1864. The largest scheme was for the 'Metropolitan District Railways' outer and inner circles. A number of rival schemes wanted to use some or all of the Kensington–City route. In the end Parliament rejected the outer circle and facilitated a single scheme linking Kensington and the City that used the best of everyone's route and linked with the Metropolitan at both ends.

Another scheme, similar in concept, was the Metropolitan Grand Union, which wanted a similar route from Kensington to the City. The Lords required the two railways to return with one scheme which would achieve the maximum benefit, and to defer the outer circle elements which they regarded as far too ambitious. Upon their return, the combined scheme was presented in the name of the Metropolitan District Railway, though the routeing between South Kensington and Westminster was borrowed from the Grand Union and took the line via Sloane Square and St James's Park rather than the more direct route first envisaged. Having complied with their lordship's wishes the scheme received the Royal Assent on 29th July 1864 and the Metropolitan District Railway (the District) came into being.

As authorised, the District was to run from a point near the Tower of London to South Kensington, at both places meeting the Metropolitan end-on. At South Kensington a branch would be formed to Warwick Road where it would divide into north- and south-facing branches that would join the West London to allow main line trains to run onto the District, retaining some advantages of its former outer circle aspirations. East of the Warwick Road junction, a north facing branch would lead to Kensington High Street, allowing through running main line trains either to reach that point or to proceed to the north part of the circle (the approaches to Kensington High Street, were the only part of the District's outer circle to survive). The Metropolitan would extend from Paddington via Kensington High Street to South Kensington, and from Moorgate via Aldgate to Tower Hill, and powers for these extensions were granted at the same time.

Construction both of the District and the Met extensions was placed in the hands of a consortium of contractors which also provided some financial support. Their tender was accepted on 23rd February 1865 and work began immediately, the whole of the works being undertaken as a single scheme, though for reasons discussed shortly contracts were only let for works west of Blackfriars.

The District portion was constructed in open-air cutting between West Brompton and a point just west of Gloucester Road, thence mainly in covered way. Unlike the Met, the District only rarely ran directly under roads, which required many properties beneath which the railway was dug to be shored or underpinned; some were demolished and rebuilt where excavation under the buildings was impracticable. Where possible construction of the covered way was undertaken in brick; this resulted in an elliptical 'tunnel' 25ft wide and 15ft 9in high. Where headroom was too restrictive for a brick arch then construction took the form of straight sided brick walls (25ft apart) with a roof supported by cast (occasionally wrought) iron girders with 13ft 6ins clearance above rail level. Nevertheless much of the route was in cutting with sloping brick walls to ensure the line was as well ventilated as possible – and necessarily so in view of the steam locomotives to be used.

The term 'covered way' is used because construction was effected directly from above as the works progressed; strictly, a tunnel is usually bored from the ends or via special access shafts. However, there was a long tunnel on the Met section north of Kensington High Street beneath Campden Hill, where the railway was so far below surface level that construction from above was impractical. This tunnel was of 421yds and took about fifteen months to build. Construction was complicated by the wet ground and fine sand through which it had to be driven; it proved very difficult to avoid serious settlement of overlying property. Owing to a strike of the miners, about 76ft of what was to have been tunnel was built as open cutting.

**This view shows the District being constructed along Victoria Street (looking east near Vauxhall Bridge Road). Most of the work was entirely manual but a steam shovel provided welcome mechanical assistance. The chaos caused to road traffic was inevitable.** LT Museum

It cannot be said that construction work was especially fast. The western section was complicated by the nature of the construction but the embankment section ought not to have been as slow as it was, which was largely deliberate. The District was finding it very difficult to raise all the required money and decided to concentrate its resources at the western end where there was the soonest prospect of running a train service and getting some revenue in. The bankruptcy in 1867 of one of the contractors was a further source of delay. The Metropolitan Board of Works presided over embankment construction and frequently urged the District to be more co-operative. The ideal, achieved only in part, was for the railway construction to be integrated with that of the Embankment. As it was, there were places where the District was excavating its tunnels in new ground only just built up behind the new wall.

During 1866 the Met and District agreed to operate their combined railways as a single network, to which end the Met contracted to work and maintain the District as each section was completed. The Met would staff, operate and maintain the entire enterprise for 45 per cent of the gross traffic receipts, the balance being paid to the District to support its heavy capital costs. The agreement could be terminated at eighteen months' notice, only to be given after the line to Westminster had been in service a year.

The Met extension and the District Railway were opened in two stages. Between Praed Street Junction (near Edgware Road) and Gloucester Road, services commenced on 1st October 1868, and on 24th December they were projected to Westminster Bridge. Trains ran at ten-minute intervals and generally all ran between Moorgate Street and Westminster Bridge calling at all stations. Trains comprised the Metropolitan's standard Beyer-Peacock 4–4–0 tank locomotives and rakes of 8-wheeled carriages. Maintenance was undertaken at the Met's sheds at Edgware Road.

Stations were opened by the Met at Paddington (Praed Street), Bayswater, Notting Hill Gate, Kensington (High Street), Gloucester Road and South Kensington. The District Railway opened stations at Sloane Square, Victoria, St James's Park and Westminster Bridge (the 'Bridge' was dropped in 1907).

Stations were standardised as far as possible. Generally the platform areas comprised an open cutting with retaining walls 50ft 5½in apart. Platforms were about 300ft long (occasionally a little longer) and surfaced of wood. Each station except Westminster Bridge was enclosed by an overall glazed wrought iron roof of elliptical section. Often the extreme platform ends were left open to allow steam and smoke to escape. Although the roofs were originally constructed with end screens they were not in fact glazed and were later removed.

The station buildings were modest affairs, all at street level, and to avoid congestion one-way flows were instigated where possible. Sometimes ticket halls were built directly above the platforms and were carried on girders, the all over roof being interrupted to accommodate the structure. In other cases they were alongside the cuttings or beyond the end of the platforms. Usually some galleries (or bridges) connected one side of the station to the other, the necessary stairways being built behind the retaining walls with openings built into the arches; in some cases one set of stairways came down right at the platform ends instead. At a few original (and some later) stations platforms were built wider and stairways came down to platform level inside the main station cutting. Where traffic was quiet only one set of stairs on each platform was actually put to use, the second set being closed off as an economy measure.

At Gloucester Road and High Street Kensington the roofs were much wider than normal as the stations had four platforms and not two. At South Kensington, where

**Gloucester Road station was owned jointly by the Metropolitan and the District. This view shows the station just prior to opening in 1868.** LT Museum

there were only two platforms, the southern side of the roof was supported on iron stanchions rather than the retaining wall as it was later intended to widen the station by providing additional platforms and a second roof. Westminster Bridge had a temporary station building at first, and was connected to Bridge Street by a passageway. Here, the station and other buildings were placed over parts of the cutting and provision of an overall roof was impractical, normal platform awnings being installed. The line stopped at a blind concrete wall at the east end of the station, protected by a pile of sleepers to act as buffers; there was no margin for error in braking, as at least one driver discovered.

From 12th April 1869 West Brompton was served, though the train service merely consisted of a single train that shuttled to Gloucester Road on a single-line basis (there was then no intermediate station). West Brompton was on the south facing link to the WLER where it had been convenient to widen its existing station. In fact, with no prospect of through main line trains, the junction at the south end of the platforms had been omitted and there was obvious reluctance to operate a service at all as traffic prospects were limited. The platforms were in the open air, and the London-bound platform was formed from a widening of the WLER 'down' platform. A second District platform was built on the east side. At opening, tracks continued beyond the station into a pair of sidings. The modest station building was situated on a widening of the Richmond Road bridge and had the usual double gallery arrangement although the stairs came down directly to the platforms rather than behind the retaining walls (this station is the only one to retain this original feature).

The West Brompton branch was the southern counterpart of the Addison Road branch, which met the WLER facing north. This was also built to receive traffic that did not at first materialise. In the case of Addison Road, the District did not have its own station and could not run trains of its own without the consent of the WLER which owned most of the track, and the West London Railway which owned the station. Sanction was sought for a terminus on the District's own land at Hammersmith Road and while it appeared on some maps, it was never built; eventually the main line companies ran their own trains from Addison Road onto the District, which answered the problem. The Addison Road and West Brompton branches converged at the Warwick Road bridge, ran parallel until Cromwell Road whence the former diverted to High Street Kensington and the latter to Gloucester Road; double junctions (known as Earl's Court Junction) were provided between the pairs of tracks to enable trains from either route to work to either of the others. This expensive infrastructure was largely redundant at first as neither Addison Road nor High Street Kensington had a regular service.

On 30th May 1870 the District completed the Thames embankment section and extended trains to Blackfriars. The station at Charing Cross (now Embankment) was of the standard type with overall roof, but the covered ways at each end were made wide enough for short lay-by tracks just ahead of each platform. At Temple the Duke of Norfolk objected to the usual arrangement and the platforms were covered over by commercial premises. A substantial pump house was required here but His Grace demanded that the flue for the steam engines was carried the entire length of the station, under the approach road and then up the rear of Norfolk House where it could not be seen; this can have done little for the steaming properties of the boilers. Nor could a standard station be constructed at Blackfriars owing to the overhead work of the London, Chatham & Dover Railway and the need to carry a large new office building over the station on heavy girders; awnings were provided over the short exposed sections.

The District Railway being built along the Embankment outside Somerset House in 1869.

On 1st August 1870 the West Brompton shuttle train was replaced by a through service of trains to and from Blackfriars, doubling the frequency of service (to 5 minutes) between Mansion House and Gloucester Road. A by-product of this was the bringing into use on a regular basis of the (District) tunnels between Gloucester Road and the double junction just west of South Kensington.

It quickly became obvious that Blackfriars was poorly located for the main City business traffic, but finding it impossible to raise additional funds there was no question of the company completing the line to Tower Hill. A modest extension to Bucklersbury (near the Mansion House) was considered, but was rejected by the House of Lords who wanted to see the line extended along the authorised route. Finally, an even more modest scheme was authorised in 1870 to a previously unplanned station at the junction of Queen Victoria and Cannon Streets; still called Mansion House the name endured, though it has long ceased to be the closest Underground station. Powers for the line further east were allowed to lapse, though Parliament forbade the District from opposing any future bill designed to complete the route, requiring it to co-operate in any new scheme.

At last, with financial resources all but exhausted, the District reached its City terminus on 3rd July 1871. Perhaps curiously it was built as a three-track terminus, with island platforms between, and was not exactly designed for the further push to the east that Parliament and others were expecting. At the west end of the platforms locomotive lay-by roads were provided, with coaling and watering facilities. Although much of the station was covered over there were large ventilators, below which platform awnings were needed. A commodious booking hall was built at street level to the north of Great Trinity Lane and extending as far as Cannon Street; this was topped by a 5-floored building, mainly let to Spiers & Pond, the restaurant operators and catering concessionaires, and included one of their restaurants. For many years the District operated a large office for the sale of season tickets from this building (such tickets could not then be purchased at stations).

**The District employed 4-wheel vehicles as it was felt they would cope better with the sharply curved track. The 2nd and 3rd class carriages (as here) had five compartments, and 1st class four. Several broadly similar batches were built during the steam era, though each differed in small details. Met and District steam stock always used characteristic round-topped doors which would not strike the tunnel wall if they came open between stations.**

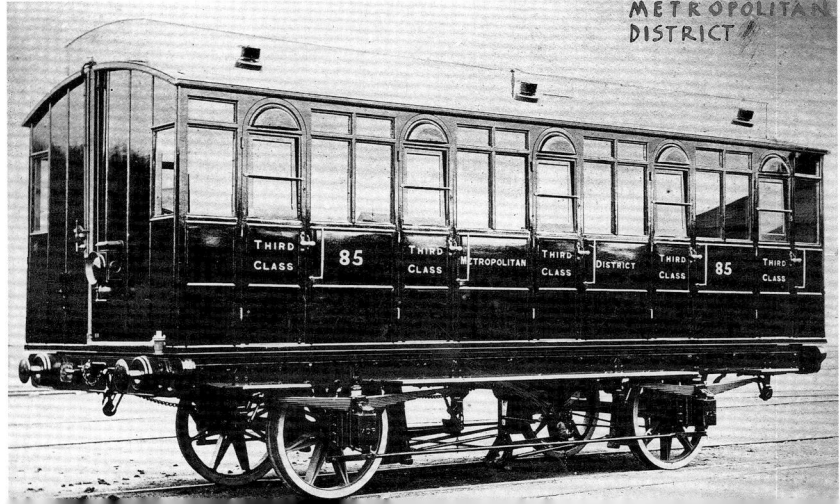

# Expansion

The District's building costs created very expensive debts, making it hard to raise further capital and causing the Met to lose interest in taking it over. Under the 1866 agreement the District also had to pay disproportionately for service improvement, holding back development. After seeking advice, the District decided to work the line itself and due notice was given to the Met that this was to take effect from 1st July 1871. To help, the District enlisted the help of James Staats Forbes – he was then traffic manager of the London, Chatham & Dover Railway and had wide railway experience. He was initially employed as Managing Director, but became Chairman within two years. The first job was to acquire locomotives, rolling stock and a workshop where they could be maintained; then recruitment and training of suitable staff.

An order was placed with the Railway Rolling Stock Company for 152 four-wheeled coaches; these were arranged into 19 eight-carriage sets, each consisting of two first, two second and four third class carriages with wooden bodies. Each was only 26ft 6ins long; the second and third class carriages comprised five somewhat basic compartments, the third class having just a layer of carpet covering the wooden seats and the second class being only modestly upholstered. First class had four larger compartments and were comfortably fitted out. Brakes were of the Westinghouse air-operated type, but not then of the automatic 'fail safe' form. Lighting was from coal gas burners, the gas being carried in bags in the roof and refilled from the gas main at Mansion House or High Street Kensington. There were curiously few mishaps from this concentration of inflammables being hauled around by the fire-breathing locomotives. In view of the satisfaction given by the Met's 4-4-0 locomotives, the District ordered 24 similar machines from Beyer-Peacock; these sufficed until 1876 when further extensions required additional machines of similar design.

West Brompton in 1876 with the West Brompton–Earl's Court shuttle train. The train is using what today is the westbound platform, though only the little-used eastbound platform had any facilities. The street level building is shown opposite. LT Museum

A long strip of land for a depot was acquired to the west of, and parallel to, the WLER north of Lillie Road. This was not a convenient arrangement. The workshops were spread out along the narrow site, and the only access was off the District tracks on the Addison Road branch just short of the junction with the WLER; trains had to be propelled out of the yard, stopping before fouling the WLER junction, and then sent on their way towards Gloucester Road. The works (known as Lillie Bridge) were not entirely finished until the middle of 1872.

Although the working agreement was intended to terminate on 1st July 1871, the first day of the District's own operation was in fact 3rd July, coinciding with the Mansion House extension. However, while the District ran the whole of the Mansion House–West Brompton service, the formative 'Inner Circle' service between Mansion House and Moorgate was necessarily shared with the Met which owned the northern and western parts of the route. By agreement the Met continued to operate all the 'Circle' trains, though in due course the District operated a proportion.

An early decision of the District was to widen South Kensington station, giving it its own independent tracks and platforms; the works were agreed in March 1871 and the contractors were asked to complete the job before 1st July, an astonishingly short time coinciding with District independent operation. The widening was done more expansively than contemplated in the 1860s and produced two District through platforms and a bay road against the south wall into which trains from the east could reverse. The Met gained a bay road with access from the west, so that trains from the Moorgate direction could terminate without trespassing onto District tracks. A second arched roof was provided, somewhat larger than the original, in order to accommodate the Met bay, while the south bay was separately roofed over and the space used for a row of shops fronting onto Pelham Street. The street-level building was also enlarged. The double junction west of the station was removed as the District and Met tracks now converged a little to the east of the enlarged station. At High Street Kensington and Gloucester Road both the Met and District had their own tracks and platforms and it was agreed all three stations should be operated jointly. The arrangement was confirmed by a 21-year agreement signed in June 1871 and costs and revenues for these 'western lines' were shared.

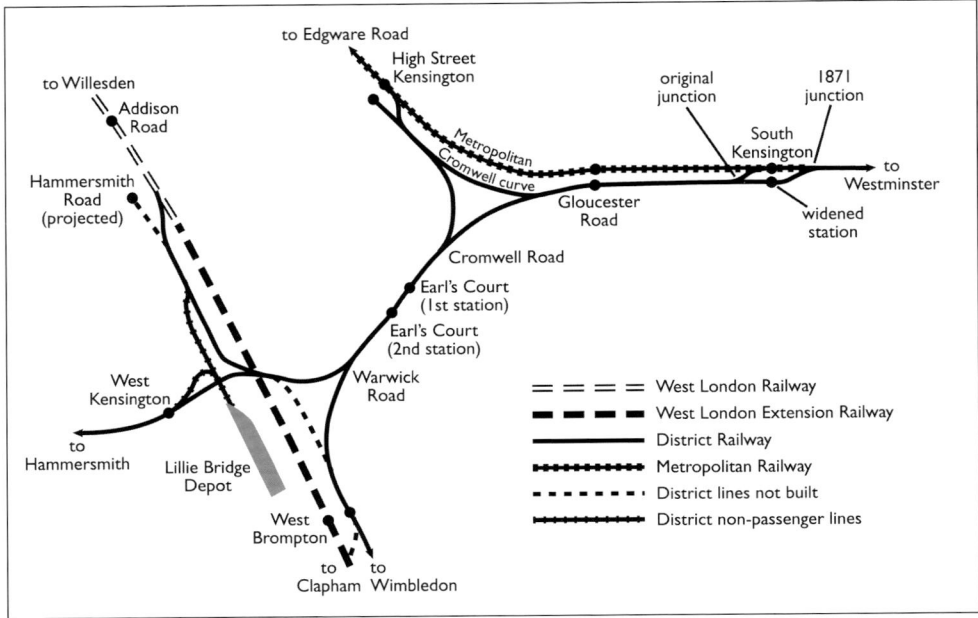

During 1870 the District also laid in on its own land a connecting line between High Street Kensington and Gloucester Road – the so-called Cromwell Curve – which duplicated the Met tracks from which they threatened to abstract revenue. Such a curve had been specifically struck out of the 1864 bill and the Met now protested, though aggravation dragged on until 1903. The line received only infrequent use.

A rare use of the curve followed the District's introduction from 1st July 1871 of an experimental service from West Brompton to Mansion House via a reversal at High Street Kensington, and this appears to have been the first time District trains served their part of that station. After withdrawal, it does not seem that regular services from High Street Kensington (District) to either West Brompton or Mansion House operated until 1880. The western curve from that station had partly been laid to facilitate construction activities but was retained in the expectation of main line traffic from Addison Road or West Brompton, in the absence of which it was not very useful.

As built, the tracks from West Brompton to Gloucester Road, and from the West London line (near Addison Road) to High Street Kensington, ran parallel to each other for a considerable distance in steep cutting held back by the usual brick retaining walls. The area was not heavily populated but a demand soon arose for a station on this section and the District responded with a station called Earl's Court (on the Earl's Court Road, to the east of the present-day bridge). As the existing cutting was not wide enough, part of the 4-track line was reduced to three, with a platform against the north wall and a further (island) platform between the two southern tracks. The station opened on 31st October 1871 though the wooden street-level building somehow caught fire on 30th December 1875 and, though badly damaged, it was evidently patched up on a temporary basis. Already the platform arrangements were proving operationally unsatisfactory and wholesale replacement (described shortly) was becoming essential.

The possibility of inaugurating circular services further out (as originally envisaged) was not entirely forgotten. The first move was from the London & North Western Railway (LNWR), which from 1st February 1872 began a half-hourly service between Broad Street station (just to the west of today's Liverpool Street main line) and Mansion House via the North London Railway, Willesden Junction, Addison Road and Earl's Court. At Mansion House the LNWR used exclusively the southern of the three platform tracks, with arrangements for coaling and watering its locomotives. The LNWR paid a premium to begin this service, known as the 'Outer Circle', but revenues were otherwise split.

From 1st August 1872 the GWR began a service from Moorgate Street to Mansion House via Paddington and the Hammersmith & City Line, thence Addison Road and Earl's Court. This route became known as the 'Middle Circle'. This time the District insisted that its own locomotives hauled the trains east of Earl's Court and no separate provision was made at Mansion House (this arrangement was altered later). These trains also ran every half-hour, operated intermediately between the LNWR trains. In 1873 the District gained powers to run its own trains over the Middle Circle but these powers (which forbade use of Addison Road as a terminus) were never exercised, though they did sometimes provide carriage stock for the GWR trains.

Anxious to capture new revenue, the District looked to the substantial town of Hammersmith, about 1½ miles west of Earl's Court and served only very indirectly by railway (about which more later). To enable capital to be raised an independent company (the Hammersmith Extension Railway) was formed by Act of Parliament on 7th July 1873; the District was to operate the line as its own and pay the new company sufficient for it to pay a dividend, making it less risky. In fact the line was taken over by the District the following year upon opening, but the shareholders' dividends were protected.

The line opened on 9th September 1874. Commencing by a junction with the Addison Road branch (where it was crossed by the WLER) it swung round to the west into a station on the North End Road called North End (Fulham) but renamed West Kensington on 1st March 1877. At the east end of the station a connection was put into the Lillie Bridge works and this soon became the main route to and from the depot. Beyond here the line gradually swung to the north-west into a station at Hammersmith Broadway. The platforms lay between retaining walls 75ft apart and occupied the length between Great Church Lane and Hammersmith Broadway.

When the Hammersmith branch opened, it appropriated the Mansion House 'through' service while the West Brompton service was replaced by a 4-carriage train that shuttled to and fro on a single line to Earl's Court where it used the southern platform. Earl's Court was quite busy by now as the shuttle's locomotives were frequently changed over here, as were those on the Middle Circle trains. These serious train working shortcomings, and lack of passenger facilities as traffic developed, all meant an entirely new station was needed. A better site was chosen, west of the Earl's Court Road bridge, and by shifting the station west it was hoped it might supersede West Brompton where passenger traffic was evidently still very light (though this was not actually done). The new station, opened on 1st February 1878, comprised four tracks with island platforms between adjacent pairs; this required widening the cutting for a considerable distance and reconstruction of the road bridge. A substantial brick station building was built across the tracks with stairways down to each platform, these being covered by a single angled roof that entirely spanned the cutting, and survives to this day.

**Still recognisable today, this view shows Earl's Court looking east in steam days.**

The opportunity was taken to rearrange all the tracks in the area so that each side of each island platform was served by trains in like direction, greatly facilitating interchange between one train and another. This required a complicated flat junction west of the station, but at the eastern end a flying junction was built near the Cromwell Road bridge whereby the down High Street line was taken under the Mansion House tracks (an expensive investment given at the time it bore no regular service). A siding was also put in at the eastern end to accommodate the various services that terminated there.

In December 1876 the District timetable offered six trains an hour between Mansion House and Aldgate via High Street Kensington (on the 'Inner Circle'); these were operated by both Metropolitan and District trains and completed each single trip in 64 minutes. There were also four trains an hour from Mansion House to Hammersmith, which took 29 minutes. In addition there were two trains an hour to Aldgate (on the 'Middle Circle' service), which took 75 minutes. Intermediately between these trains there were two LNWR trains an hour between Mansion House and Broad Street (on the 'Outer Circle'); these reached Willesden Junction in 37 minutes but did not run on Sundays. In total this offered 14 trains an hour between Mansion House and Gloucester Road, averaging a 4¼-minute service. The West Brompton shuttle usually operated three times an hour, four in rush hours, though from 1877 the fourth train was cut. With that brief exception, the same basic service operated all day, with no variation at 'busy' times. As was usual in those days the Sunday service was suspended for two hours between 11am and 1pm on Sundays (the 'Church Break'), so that the staff had the opportunity for spiritual refreshment (though other refreshment was probably more popular) – this practice lasted until July 1903.

Keen to attract new traffic the District eyed up the south-western suburbs and on 10th August 1872, it obtained powers for a Metropolitan & South-Western Junction Railway. Just under three miles long, this was to begin near the Warwick Road bridge at Earl's Court, proceed beneath the WLER, then run via Fulham (on a route that would have been somewhat to the north of the present Putney line), a bridge over the Thames to Putney, thence to Barnes LSWR station which would be enlarged and where a junction would be made. The Ecclesiastical Commissioners demanded a station on Fulham Palace Road and an ornamental viaduct on land near the Fulham Palace. Another station was projected on the North End Road. The Act envisaged the District might run the line but in the event these powers lapsed after less expensive schemes presented themselves.

The District in fact headed for Richmond; that it could achieve this at low cost was because it was able to run over another railway whose history is now relevant. Richmond had been served from Clapham and Barnes since 1846, but the LSWR obtained Parliamentary approval on 14th July 1864 for a second route running a little to the north of the Thames. The starting point was Addison Road, to which it was already running a service from Clapham via the West London Extension Railway. Second thoughts about a proposed liaison with the Hammersmith & City Railway (H&CR) resulted in a further Act (with a revised route to Hammersmith) in June 1865, with yet more modifications authorised on 13th July 1867. After that, construction was rapid, the line opening on 1st January 1869.

The line left the West London Railway at a junction north of Addison Road, then a graceful curve (mainly in shallow cutting) took it due south immediately after crossing beneath the Hammersmith & City line viaduct north of Hammersmith. It then rose onto viaduct and swung west, proceeding on viaduct or embankment towards Chiswick, thence south-west to cross the River Thames at Kew and reach its terminus at Richmond. Stations were built at Hammersmith (Grove Road) (where there was a footbridge connection to the H&CR station), Turnham Green (the only significant community immediately west of Hammersmith), Brentford Road (Gunnersbury from 1st November 1871), and Kew Gardens. Each station was in similar unornamented style, though at Kew Gardens a licensed refreshment room was provided for trippers to the Gardens where the owners did as little as possible to provide any creature comforts for visitors. The railway north of Kew was carried over the Thames by a massive 5-span lattice girder bridge with minor ornamentation as a minimal concession to the environmental attack it received. Rapid housing development along the line spawned new stations at Shepherd's Bush from 1st May 1874 and Shaftesbury Road from 1st April 1873 (this became Ravenscourt Park on 1st March 1888).

At Richmond the existing LSWR station was then west of Kew Road and a new station was provided to its east, north of the main line. The station had three notoriously low platforms serving six tracks and access to and from trains was subject to much comment and some accidents, after which they were raised. At Brentford Road there was a junction north of the station to a link with the North & South Western Junction Railway at South Acton (today's North London Line) so LNWR trains from Broad Street could use the Brentford Road–Richmond section of the new line – this service and a circuitous LSWR Waterloo via Addison Road service started on opening day (there was also a bizarre service to Ludgate Hill via Addison Road and Loughborough Junction). North of Grove Road there was a running connection with the H&CR allowing Metropolitan and GWR trains access to the new line, though it was not at first used (a GWR service from Paddington to Richmond via the H&CR began on 1st June 1870).

17

The LSWR line offered an economical way for the District to strike westwards to develop new traffic; all that would be needed was a link between the railways at Hammersmith. The District's Act of 11th August 1875 secured authority for the link, and gave running powers over the Kensington–Richmond line west of Hammersmith in exchange for abandoning the Barnes line already described (or any similar lines to Richmond or beyond in the future).

The half-mile link was complicated by the need to get the District from its own station at Hammersmith (in a cutting) to LSWR viaduct level, at the same time getting under Hammersmith Broadway and under or over some other roads. The District station (though new) was widened to provide terminal platforms on the north side, and through platforms (with three faces) on the south side; the enlarged station was probably all of wood as it burnt down in January 1882 and took seven months to repair.

Opened on 1st June 1877, the link ran north-west under the Broadway and curved west, rising steeply, to viaduct level where there was a junction. To avoid obstructing the roads that had to be crossed on the incline, road and pavement levels were dropped substantially. The Richmond service was operated by projecting some of the Hammersmith–Mansion House service, just one train an hour off-peak, and two during peak hours. Traffic levels rose quickly, to the District's relief, though the Met (to the District's irritation) began a through service from Moorgate Street (later from Aldgate) to Richmond from 1st October 1877.

An intriguing 'outer' Outer Circle came to operate briefly. The Midland Railway had access to the District from Cricklewood via Dudding Hill, Acton, Acton Lane Junction and the LSWR at Hammersmith. During 1876 it negotiated running powers to carry coal traffic over the District both to High Street and South Kensington, where it intended to build depots (the latter never constructed, West Kensington being chosen instead); running powers for passenger trains were also obtained to South Kensington.

From 1st May 1878 the Midland used this route to operate a service from St Pancras to Earl's Court (being more convenient than South Kensington). This twice-hourly service finished on 30th September 1880 and was probably little patronised. Through tickets to the Midland via this route (requiring a change at Gunnersbury) were continued for many years, finally disappearing in 1902.

The Midland was more persistent with its coal and goods interests, depots coming into use in 1878 at West Kensington (next to Lillie Bridge, and on District Railway land) and at High Street Kensington. At High Street the trains had to reverse in the western platform and the trucks had to be propelled up a steep gradient to the depot, which was at street level. Both the depots continued to operate into British Railways days, High Street closing in 1963 and West Kensington in 1965.

Although the District did not own the Kensington & Richmond line, it was to be the springboard for its own branches to the north and west, via the rapidly developing Chiswick area. Ealing, the nearest large town, was slowly developing (and ripe for very much more) and offered a useful connection with the GWR. The District obtained powers in 1877 for a line to Ealing from a junction with the LSWR west of Turnham Green station, three miles distant. Ealing station was opposite Haven Green, just north of the GWR station. The powers included a running connection from the District into the GWR station at its east end, though this was not put in until later.

The Ealing extension opened on 1st July 1879 with intermediate stations at Acton Green (Chiswick Park and Acton Green from 1887), Mill Hill Park (Acton Town from 1st March 1910) and Ealing Common. The District's arrival certainly initiated more vigorous property development in the whole area, but even Ealing Broadway was hardly

The platforms at Mill Hill Park prior to electrification, looking east. The station (now Acton Town) is very different today, having been substantially rebuilt in 1910 and again in 1932.

overtaxed for some years and staff reminisced of a station in the 1880s still with a distinct 'country' feel. This station had a protective train shed over part of its two platform roads and a substantial station building, though the other stations were more modest with small buildings and canopied platforms.

With no prospect of any link at West Brompton with the WLER the only real option was to extend in order to tap the traffic in the rapidly developing Fulham area. An Act was obtained on 4th July 1878 for a line as far as the Thames, and construction was undertaken by Lucas & Aird.

View of 'The Parade', opposite Haven Green, at Ealing Broadway. This view in 1903 shows the District station with advertising slightly more restrained than within built-up London. A busy cab rank (still there today) facilitated onward travel. LT Museum

The extension opened on 1st March 1880, in time for the District to reap the traffic revenue from the University Boat Race on 22nd March. Stations were provided at Walham Green (Fulham Broadway from 2nd March 1952), Parsons Green and Putney Bridge & Fulham (a name intended to imply Putney, but was actually in Fulham). The latter was renamed Putney Bridge & Hurlingham on 1st September 1902, with the suffix lost in 1932. The line was in cutting or tunnel south of West Brompton where it dived under the WLER, then rose to viaduct level after Walham Green. Station buildings were substantial and the line terminated abruptly near, and at right angles, to the Thames making future intentions obvious. The Putney train service was initially half-hourly to Mansion House, but as it developed gratifyingly fast it was supplemented from 1st April 1880 by a half-hourly service to High Street Kensington. This seems to have been the first regular service to the District's part of the station at High Street and was the origin of today's Wimbledon–Edgware Road service.

To tap the then busy steamboat market the District built its own pier at Putney Bridge with footpath link direct to the station. For many years through tickets were issued to and from boats; in 1897 arrangements existed with the Thames Steamboat Company where each issued through tickets covering rail and boat journeys. Rail tickets were obtainable for journeys between Putney Bridge and Whitechapel while the boat portion was obtainable for use on the Kew, Richmond and Hampton Court boats, the latter also serving Teddington. At that time similar tickets were available for travel via Hammersmith Pier and in both cases the service did not operate during winter months.

The District's final westerly expansion during this period was via the Hounslow & Metropolitan Railway, which was a slight anomaly. This railway was promoted quite independently by local landowners anxious for improved transport in the area. An Act was obtained in 1866 for a line from a junction with the projected Acton & Brentford Railway (authorised 1865 with powers renewed in 1868) to a terminus in Hounslow on the Bath Road; there was to have been a branch from a point near Syon Lane to meet the Brentford Dock branch of the GWR. In the event the powers lay dormant, no doubt largely because the Acton & Brentford line was never built.

The arrival of the District in the Acton area provided an alternative opportunity, and a revived Hounslow & Metropolitan Railway was authorised in August 1880 with the old powers abandoned (though the western end of the route was retained largely unchanged). The near $5\frac{1}{2}$-mile line was to begin by a junction with the District just west of its Mill Hill Park station and proceed in a broadly south-westerly direction to the Bath Road terminus to be known as Hounslow Barracks (there was a considerable military presence in the area then). Intermediate stations were to be built at South Ealing, Boston Road and Spring Grove. An agreement for the District to work the line was made on 3rd June 1880 with the District retaining half of the gross receipts.

There were second thoughts about the utility of the line. In order better to serve the town of Hounslow, and to tap the area to the south, the new company sought to build a line from a point west of Spring Grove station to a station on the London Road itself, known as Hounslow Town. The powers were granted on 29th June 1883 and also authorised a triangular junction near Mill Hill Park that would have allowed direct running towards Ealing, but this was never built. Powers were refused for extension beyond Hounslow Town into LSWR territory, making the branch of limited use only.

In the mistaken belief that powers would be forthcoming for extension towards Whitton and Teddington, land as far as Hounslow Town was purchased in 1882 with construction soon in hand, the line from Mill Hill Park to Hounslow Town opening on

**Hounslow Barracks station c.1916. The station building was replaced in 1931.** LT Museum

1st May 1883. The railway was double line throughout and the stations were well built with small brick buildings and canopied platforms (Boston Manor is typical of the style and is comparatively unchanged at platform level). The station at Hounslow Town was on Viaduct ending abruptly at right angles to the road and clearly poised for expansion in a southerly direction.

The Barracks line opened on 21st July 1884 and was only single track throughout from a point immediately west of the junction with the Town branch (at Lampton Junction). In fact expectations were so low that only a shuttle service operated between Hounslow Barracks and Spring Grove station, at which sidings were now installed between the running lines just east of the station where the shuttle could be turned round. At first, Hounslow Town trains worked to Mansion House but traffic was very slow to develop and the service was soon cut back to Mill Hill Park where trains connected into and from London trains, though a few branch trains ran through to Earl's Court. When the Hounslow Barracks branch came into use, trains connected at Osterley to and from the Mill Hill Park service until the 'Town' branch closed, when all trains ran through to Mill Hill Park. With traffic so light, two branches could not be afforded. From 31st March 1886 the Mill Hill Park service was switched to Hounslow Barracks and Hounslow Town station was closed and remained derelict for some years.

**A new station, called Heston-Hounslow, was opened on the single line where it crossed the Lampton Road; the single platform straddled the bridge on space left for a possible second track on the south side. The poor traffic was probably a result of the paltry shuttle train service, which was generally only one an hour; two in the peaks.** LT Museum

The final thrust of the District during this period took the Fulham branch across the Thames. The first relevant scheme was a proposed Guildford, Kingston & London Railway, promoted by Kingston and Surbiton interests disenchanted with the LSWR. The line was to run from Guildford via Cobham, Claygate, Long Ditton, Surbiton, Norbiton, across Wimbledon Common and Putney Heath and across the Thames at Putney to make an end-on junction with the District at Fulham, resulting from which the District took an active interest in the line. When powers were finally obtained on 22nd August 1881 the scheme was much simplified, and the LSWR had taken over the Surbiton–Guildford portion, opening it in its name in 1885.

The residual Kingston & London Railway was to be a 7½-mile line from Fulham (Putney Bridge) to Surbiton to which the District would have running powers; the LSWR would have running powers to Putney Bridge and thence over the District to South Kensington and High Street Kensington. It was contemplated one or other of these railways would work the line. The route, traversing Putney Heath and Wimbledon Common, was somewhat controversial.

Both the District and LSWR sought to reduce the influence of the independent promoters and obtained a further Act on 18th August 1882 which dissolved the Kingston & London and transferred the powers to a joint committee of the District and LSWR with minor deviations to the route. By an Act of the same date the Wimbledon & West Metropolitan Junction Railway was formed with a route from Wimbledon to meet the Kingston line a little to the south of Putney; this too was sponsored by the District and LSWR. This line joined the Tooting–Wimbledon line by what was to have been a triangular junction north-east of Wimbledon, but the Tooting-facing junction had been struck out.

Some preliminary work on the Kingston & London had by this time started but the District's finances were in a terrible state and financial support collapsed and construction never really got going. In the end matters were resolved by the LSWR Act of 25th June 1886 whereby the Kingston's Putney–Surbiton section was abandoned and the short section between the District at Fulham and a point just south of East Putney station, together with the entire Wimbledon & West Metropolitan Junction Railway, were transferred to the LSWR. The District received running powers to Wimbledon and the LSWR retained its to the two Kensington stations, the latter never exercised. In addition, the Act rearranged the southern end of the line so that instead of crossing the LSWR main line to join the line from Tooting, it stayed on the west side and ran into new terminal platforms suitable for the (mainly) District terminating trains, though a junction with the main line tracks was installed just north of the station for LSWR through trains.

What had become known as the Wimbledon & Fulham line was opened by the LSWR on 3rd June 1889. Intermediate stations were built at East Putney, Southfields and Wimbledon Park. The latter two (unusually for that time) were island platforms, but East Putney had two side platforms on the main line and two more on a connecting link to the LSWR 'Windsor' lines at Point Pleasant where a flying junction was formed; the main line and the link converged at a junction just south of East Putney. The link line came into use on 1st July and saw regular but not very frequent all-stations passenger trains from Waterloo to Wimbledon until 1941 after which the 'east' platforms at East Putney became derelict. The line was (and still is) used for main line empty stock moves and as an emergency diversionary route.

To develop traffic the District wanted to push beyond Ealing and it made repeated attempts for powers to extend to Uxbridge (the GWR, which then had a station in that town, was particularly antagonistic). In January 1883 the GWR agreed to allow District trains to operate over its system via a junction just east of Ealing Broadway station and from 1st March 1883, a number of District trains from Mansion House was projected to Windsor, calling all stations. The service was not heavily used, nor was the District's 4-wheeled coaching stock well suited for this type of service, and at the GWR's request the service ceased after 30th September 1885, though the junction remained for some years.

The various extensions required adjustments to the train services, though the various 'Circles' remained at six per hour on the 'Inner' and two an hour each on the 'Middle' and 'Outer'. Of the four 'Districts' an hour between Mansion House and Hammersmith, one (two in rush hours) was extended to Richmond upon its opening, and two were sent to Ealing upon its opening in 1879. When the through service to Putney began on 1st March 1880 two additional trains an hour were run from Mansion House to service the branch, the first augmentation of the service between Mansion House and Gloucester Road. The Putney–High Street service also ran at half-hourly intervals when it began in April.

Until 1880 the basic service pattern was static throughout the day (except for peak augmentation to Richmond), thus west of Earl's Court trains were infrequent and a published timetable was needed, though adopting 'clockface' departures. During 1880 increasing traffic resulted in modest augmentation of services during the rush hours, mainly by introducing short workings to or from Mansion House and South Kensington or Gloucester Road.

When the Windsor service began, the through trains ran on an hourly basis (leaving the District station at Ealing served by only one train an hour), though it was cut back to just four trains a day in October 1884, making this short-lived service even less attractive.

Both the District and Great Western approached Ealing Broadway in cutting. When the junction between the two was put in, the earth barrier between the two cuttings was breached to install this very sharp reverse curve double junction, shown in this admittedly poor quality but rare view probably taken around 1890. When the Ealing and Shepherds Bush Railway arrived in 1920 it required removal of the remainder of the dividing earth barrier so it could squeeze between the older two railways.

# A Circle Completed

Once the District reached Mansion House in 1871, attempts to extend further east to complete the Inner Circle collapsed completely; the proposed route was expensive and adequate returns were uncertain, so efforts were focused at the western end. The Met was in a better position and (under parliamentary pressure) reached Aldgate on 18th November 1876. Aldgate was the final station on its own portion.

City interests were frustrated with this impasse and formed an independent company to complete the link which received Parliamentary sanction on 7th August 1874 as the Inner Circle Completion Company. A further Act of 1876 extended the time limit for acquiring the property and acknowledged an agreement of 28th March 1876 by which the District would work the new railway on the same basis as other parts of its Inner Circle.

Unfortunately, the Completion Company was unable to raise the necessary finance. The District and Met eventually concluded that they might as well co-operate in the completion of the Circle and jointly formed a Metropolitan & District (City Lines & Extensions) Railway (CLER) by an Act of that name on 11th August 1879; this effectively replaced the earlier Completion Company's enterprise and the new Act provided for the cancellation of its powers, compensation for costs expended, and eventual winding up. However work was slow to start.

In 1881 the Metropolitan decided it was necessary to press on to Trinity Square and build its own station there, only 200 yards or so short of the joint station at Mark Lane. Parliamentary authority was obtained that June for the Metropolitan to exploit the CLER powers for this section; work proceeded briskly and the extension opened on 25th September 1882. The new station was called 'Tower of London'; the act required the station and line to Aldgate to become part of the joint line when the remaining part opened, and for the District to agree the station arrangements, though there is suspicion it was never actually asked.

Completing the circle was expensive given property prices along the route and since the new line was parallel to and less than half a mile from the existing Met route, traffic threatened to be relatively light. To help find new traffic, a south-eastern extension was authorised in 1879 for a connection from both the Met (north of Aldgate) and the CLER (south of Aldgate) to meet the East London Railway (ELR) at a point a little to the south of its Whitechapel station. This was also helpful to the ELR, which was keen to develop traffic. The ELR had capacity to spare and was a jointly-controlled enterprise running from the New Cross stations on the London Brighton & South Coast and the South Eastern railways to a junction with the Great Eastern not far from Liverpool Street. After much haggling between the various authorities involved (as several new streets were also covered by the enabling Act), work finally began in 1882.

The CLER opened in its entirety on 6th October 1884 and at last the Inner Circle was complete. Stations were provided at Cannon Street, Monument, Mark Lane, Aldgate East and St Mary's. In fact St Mary's had opened on 3rd March 1884 with a temporary service of South Eastern Railway trains from Addiscombe via the ELR. The

South Kensington District platforms looking west. The Metropolitan bay road is visible on the right (with bridge across track when platform was not in use) and separate Metropolitan platforms and roof on extreme right. The open space beyond the stairs is where the old junction with the Metropolitan was located before the station was widened. LT Museum

northern arm of what became known as the Aldgate triangle, though built by the CLER, was transferred to the ownership of the Met. Similarly the Met's hastily built section from Aldgate to the Tower was transferred to the CLER. The latter's station at Mark Lane was close to the Tower station which became quite superfluous and was closed from 13th October 1884, though it was to be revived some eighty years later.

Mansion House required rearrangement and substantial enlargement. The northern island platform and northern bay remained largely unscathed, with the former middle road projected through the headwall to become the new eastbound line. The entire station site was widened considerably on the southern side with the old southern island removed and a new one inserted sufficiently to the south to serve a new westbound platform on its northern face and a new bay road on the other, giving four platform faces in all. On the extreme south side was a further siding. The south bay and south siding were used by LNWR Outer Circle trains. With the demolition of the concourse at the eastern end new stairs were needed to connect the ticket hall with the southern platforms; one of these ran via a lengthy bridge across the new running lines at an angle.

At platform level Cannon Street, Monument, Mark Lane, Aldgate East and St Mary's stations were similar. Station buildings were constructed at each site except Cannon Street, where the booking hall was eased into the space under the main line station forecourt and a glazed brick interchange passage was built for interchange traffic to the South Eastern Railway. Financially the CLER was disastrously expensive, with new traffic failing to develop; for many years it was a loss-making burden on the District's already shaky books.

The District was uneasy about its eastern outlet being confined to the East London Railway, which also missed the busy Whitechapel area. Before construction of the CLER began, it obtained powers for a short branch line from a point just east of St Mary's at a sharp junction (painfully obvious today) to a terminal station just north of Whitechapel Road. This District-owned section opened with the rest of the CLER. Whitechapel station comprised two open air platform tracks astride an island platform, the southern track with an engine run-round loop, and locomotive coaling and watering sidings at the west end.

When the CLER opened, District services were divided between Whitechapel and the ELR, though frequencies and the service split varied over the years. At first the Inner Circle service (now, for the first time, a 'circular' service) was augmented to eight trains an hour, mainly at 6-minute intervals with one gap of nine minutes each half hour. Two trains an hour operated from New Cross to Putney and two from New Cross to Hammersmith. In addition there were four trains between Whitechapel and Hammersmith, two of which went on to Ealing and one (two in peaks) to Richmond. The Middle and Outer Circles were as before (each half-hourly from Mansion House). This produced twenty trains an hour between Mansion House and Gloucester Road – a three-minute interval service which was evidently found difficult to operate.

After only a month the Ealing service was altered to run from New Cross, with Hammersmith, Putney and Richmond trains starting at Whitechapel. This reduced the service from the ELR (to match limited demand) and reduced the paths on the District to eighteen an hour. The Inner Circle service was recast for 22 trains instead of 20, with a significantly increased running time; the anti-clockwise service was now run by seven District trains and four Met, while the clockwise service was entirely Met operated. The Inner Circle still proved troublesome to operate and was cut back to six trains an hour from April 1885, at which level it remained until 1908.

**View of Whitechapel looking east while closed for reconstruction. The original platforms are on the left and the new pair may be seen on the right. The signalbox (on the left) is partly situated behind the retaining wall and is still in use today.** Railway Magazine

Whitechapel station in the 1890s. The East London Railway station is immediately to the right and was later altered to serve both railways. LT Museum

The few Earl's Court workings from the Hounslow line were gradually augmented until April 1886 when they were all cut back to Mill Hill Park again. By that time additional trains were running from the eastern termini to Hammersmith. When the Putney–Wimbledon section opened the existing Whitechapel–Putney trains (two an hour) were projected south, the High Street service still terminating at Putney Bridge.

All these extensions required considerably more rolling stock. Twenty-nine new locomotives were constructed between 1876 and 1886, bringing the total up to 54. These were all broadly similar to the 1871 machines. Coaching stock was reinforced by successive deliveries of 9-carriage trains in 1879 (four), 1881, 1883 and 1884 (six in each year) and 1891 (two). Carriages remained 4-wheel and were broadly similar to those of 1871 but with later refinements such as all-iron underframes. The formations were as in 1871 but with an extra second-class coach.

Braking was improved initially with the Westinghouse straight air brake and finally with that company's automatic air brake. The new coaches were equipped with compressed oil-gas lighting on the Pintsch system which was more satisfactory than coal gas. The earlier coaches were gradually modernised to match. Penny-in-the-slot electric reading lamps were also tested at one point, passengers being expected to pay for enhanced lighting; this was optimistic and short-lived. At the end of the century, 'Stone's' electric lighting was tested (using dynamos and batteries), but by then electric traction was looming and widespread conversion was not pursued. From October 1895 the carriages were gradually fitted with ingenious mechanical indicators that announced the next station (or, between stations, displayed advertisements), but being found unreliable were soon removed.

After initial investigation by the Met, several ideas emerged to connect the ailing CLER with the nearby London Tilbury & Southend Railway (LTSR) to provide a useful eastern outlet. Whitechapel was not a satisfactory eastern terminus for the District as the traffic offering was small in relation to the potential train capacity available. Equally the LTSR was heavily constrained by the limited capacity of its antiquated terminus at Fenchurch Street, which had for some time been incapable of handling more peak trains. For these reasons they came to support a nominally independent scheme for what became known as the Whitechapel & Bow Railway (WBR) which obtained its Act in August 1897. Though the line was still independent at that time, the Act made provision for it to be worked by the District or LTSR (or both) and in the following year the railway was taken over by those companies jointly.

The line began at the east end of Whitechapel station and proceeded under Whitechapel Road and Mile End Road to Bow Road, beyond which it rose to the surface to meet the LTSR at a junction by Campbell Road. Intermediate stations were built at Stepney Green, Mile End and Bow Road. Whitechapel required lengthening and enlargement (to accommodate a second island platform on the south side), and increasing in level to clear the East London Railway which it bridged at the east end. The control of Whitechapel station (but not the District's connection with the CLER at the west end) was vested in the WBR and to facilitate reconstruction it was closed from 2nd February 1902. The intermediate stations had substantial brick buildings and (like Whitechapel) very long platforms (450 ft) to be able to accommodate LTSR trains.

The WBR was opened on 2nd June 1902 with trains from the District running to East Ham on the LTSR. Whitechapel and Mile End stations opened that day, but Bow Road opened on 11th and Stepney Green on 23rd June. All trains were operated by the District (although the LTSR owned three of the six new trains required).

The LTSR had its own complex history. It had opened in 1854 with a line starting at Forest Gate (on the Eastern Counties Railway) and took a route via Barking and Tilbury towards Southend. In 1856 a link was constructed from the London & Blackwall Railway (at Gas Factory Junction, in Bow) to Barking to provide the LTSR with a direct route from Fenchurch Street. Intermediate stations were built at Bromley, Plaistow and East Ham and the new line met the old outside Barking, just east of the River Roding. A few additional stations were later added: Plaistow on 31st March 1858, Upton Park in 1877 and West Ham on 1st February 1901. All stations were standard twin-platform affairs except West Ham which had an island. The LTSR route via Tilbury was excellent for serving the docks but a roundabout way of getting to Southend; in consequence a further cut-off was built between Barking and Pitsea which opened as far as Upminster on 1st May 1885 with intermediate stations at Dagenham (Dagenham East from 1st May 1949), and Hornchurch. The line was projected to East Horndon (now, curiously, West Horndon) on 1st May 1886 and after much struggling the final section to Pitsea was completed on 1st June 1888.

The District link placed considerable pressure on LTSR facilities which had immediately to be adapted – the 2-track section between Campbell Road and Barking was unable to cope for long with the rapidly developing traffic. Track quadrupling was required but these works are described later as they became enmeshed with electrification works.

Most District trains terminated at East Ham as the tracks beyond were very congested, but one train each morning and evening was projected to Upminster. The morning train (which left Upminster at 7.57) ran non-stop between East Ham and Bow Road in seven minutes, taking 54 minutes to reach Charing Cross from Upminster (only one minute longer than a train a century later).

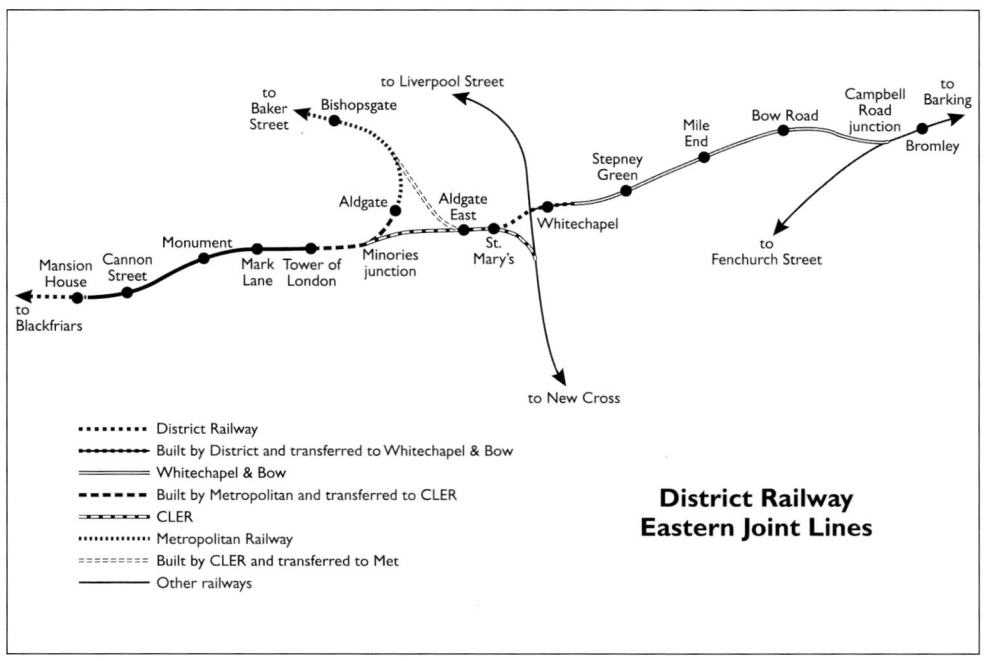

**District Railway Eastern Joint Lines**

East Ham platforms at around the time the District Railway began operating trains and just prior to widening (which took place here on the south side, on the right of the platforms shown). *Railway Magazine*

The June 1902 timetable shows the off peak service offering an irregular 2–3 trains an hour service from East Ham, augmented by trains from Bow Road or New Cross to produce a 10-minute service west of St Mary's. This meshed with a similar interval service on the Inner Circle west of Minories Junction and with the half-hourly Outer Circle services that started at Mansion House (the GWR Middle Circle trains were cut back to Earl's Court from 1st July 1900 – they were withdrawn altogether from 31st January 1905); the combined interval between Mansion House and Gloucester Road was slightly irregular, but gave a train approximately every four minutes. The half-hourly New Cross trains worked alternately to Hammersmith or Richmond, the Bow Road and East Ham trains together offered half-hourly services to Ealing or Wimbledon.

During the peaks the half-hourly trains from New Cross all worked to Richmond, Bow Road workings were projected back from East Ham and central area services were slightly augmented by a few short workings, such as Whitechapel to Chiswick Park, producing a 3–4 minute service.

Although much development was latterly concentrated at the District's eastern end, further north-western expansion remained an aspiration. Uxbridge was coveted; it was poorly served by a GWR branch from West Drayton and deserved better. Then there was Harrow – imperfectly served by the Metropolitan (from August 1880). Serving both wasn't easy as they were not in a direct line from Ealing.

Some of the terrain was far from flat, but there was a natural route through a Harrow–Alperton axis which had attracted railway bills regularly since 1864. The District finally decided to survey a route to Uxbridge, via Alperton, in November 1892 and a scheme was prepared for the first part of the route as far as Roxeth (near Harrow Hill, but on the opposite side from the Met). A bill was presented in the name of a nominally independent Ealing & South Harrow Railway (ESHR), though it provided for the District to work the line; the District eventually provided some critical capital too. The line was to run from a triangular junction with the District at Hanger Lane via intermediate stations at North Ealing, Alperton, Sudbury Town and Sudbury Hill.

For all practical purposes the ESHR was now a District enterprise, though with so little immediate prospect of generating traffic no work was started. In 1895 the District sought to interest a projected London & South Wales Railway in using its metals by offering to meet it at High Wycombe and carry its trains via Uxbridge and along the ESHR and District to South Kensington, where a terminus would be built at Pelham Place. Unfortunately for the District that scheme failed to mature: the District was on its own.

Preliminary work began in 1897 and construction proper started in early 1899. The nature of the yellow clay in the area slowed construction down (not helped by exceptionally wet weather) and extra land was needed to give the banks and cuttings the necessary stability. The Ealing Broadway–North Ealing curve was omitted, so the new line would have to be operated as an alternative branch to Ealing Broadway, which was perhaps unhelpful given the small traffic prospects.

Although practically complete at the end of 1899 the line remained unfinished and unopened – the dire state of the District's financial affairs meant it could not afford to operate near-empty trains. It was during that year that the question of possible District electrification was being addressed and this may have bolstered a decision to delay things, for reasons covered later.

Before the ESHR difficulties manifested themselves the District's aspiration to reach Uxbridge needed to be sated. As mentioned, the District had already surveyed the route but no bill was deposited at that time. In 1896 practical moves were required and the District deposited a bill for a line making an end-on junction with the ESHR at Roxeth (or South Harrow, as the District preferred to call its station) and thence to High Wycombe, via Ruislip and Uxbridge (where it would now link with an Uxbridge & Rickmansworth scheme). Great Western opposition saw off the Wycombe section but the line from South Harrow to Uxbridge was authorised in 1897, creating another nominally independent company, the Harrow & Uxbridge Railway (HUR).

As usual, fund-raising proved difficult, not helped by much of the route being thinly populated. The Metropolitan Railway offered to rescue the scheme (it had itself had eyes on Uxbridge, having promoted an unsuccessful bill in 1881) and with the District's reluctant support, an Act of 1899 was passed which authorised a link from Harrow-on-the-Hill (Metropolitan) to a junction with the HUR at the then remote Rayners Lane. The Met took over the HUR powers but the District retained limited running powers for up to three passenger trains per hour between South Harrow and Uxbridge (the South Harrow section, though not on the route from Harrow-on-the-Hill, was still required to be built by the Met). Construction work started in 1901 and took about three years. The Metropolitan service from Harrow to Uxbridge eventually began on 4th July 1904 but the District had to wait longer to reach Uxbridge.

In its 1878 Act the District successfully sought powers for what was described as the Acton Loop Line, which was a branch that was to diverge from the District by an east-facing junction to the south east of Mill Hill Park and curve north alongside the North & South West Junction Railway (NSWJR) where it would form a junction north of South Acton station. Lack of urgent need, higher priorities elsewhere and dwindling cash meant nothing was done and the powers were renewed in 1880 and 1882 but lapsed in 1885 although the land had been purchased. Powers were revived in 1887, renewed again in 1889, 1893 and 1896 (until 1898). Presumably not daring to go back to Parliament again the District finally put the work in hand during 1897 and Messrs J. C. Wills & Sons got on with the job of construction, which was finished in February 1899. The result was a fully-signalled double track railway, a little over half a mile long, with double junctions at either end. The line crossed Bollo Lane on a steel bridge then ran on an embankment that dropped down to meet the level of the NSWJR at the north end of South Acton station. The main shortcoming of the line was that the District was not disposed to open it to traffic. However it did see service from 15th May 1899 when contractor's trains used it in connection with the construction of the ESHR – these operated at night and were provided by both the Midland and LNWR; after that it lay moribund, and the story is taken up later.

Before looking at the electrification and rejuvenation of the District there are some aspects of its operation during steam days that help describe something of the character of the line.

When the District opened it adopted much the same ticket system as other railway companies, with each station holding a full stock of tickets for every journey and type of travel. Because of the Inner Circle relationship with the Met, through tickets were issued both to and from Met stations as well. Through tickets were soon added for journeys onto other railways, not by any means simply the stations District trains happened to serve. To some extent the provision of through tickets was the cheap alternative to building an extension, and it is interesting to see the District offering through tickets to the LSWR via West Brompton from as early as 1872, and to Reading on the GWR from 1873. There was never a time when the District had through fares to every main line station though.

The District also sold tickets off their own premises. For example there was a short-lived ticket office at Louis Tussaud's waxworks in Regent Street, opened on 9th February 1891, though the waxworks burnt down on 20th June. The District also had an arrangement dated 25th August 1891 for the Army & Navy Stores to sell the full range of tickets (and maps and timetables) from their Victoria Street store, though in that case the store sold tickets for many other railways as well.

The District and Met were keen to ensure that passengers using the Inner Circle only travelled in the direction specifically covered by the ticket, so the revenue split was accurate (as well as favouring the issuing company where there was practical choice). To aid ticket examination, tickets were overprinted with a large red I (for inner rail, or anti-clockwise journeys) or an O for travel the other way (on the outer rail). A few journeys were permissible either way and were overprinted E. The District also used overprints to identify destinations; tickets therefore received a single or double letter code denoting destination station. These letters were in outline form and the double letters were intertwined. These systems went out of use around electrification. The District eventually made season tickets available from a dedicated sales office at Mansion House, though as demand grew it was eventually agreed to keep season ticket stock at stations.

1880s poster for District Railway services.
LT Museum

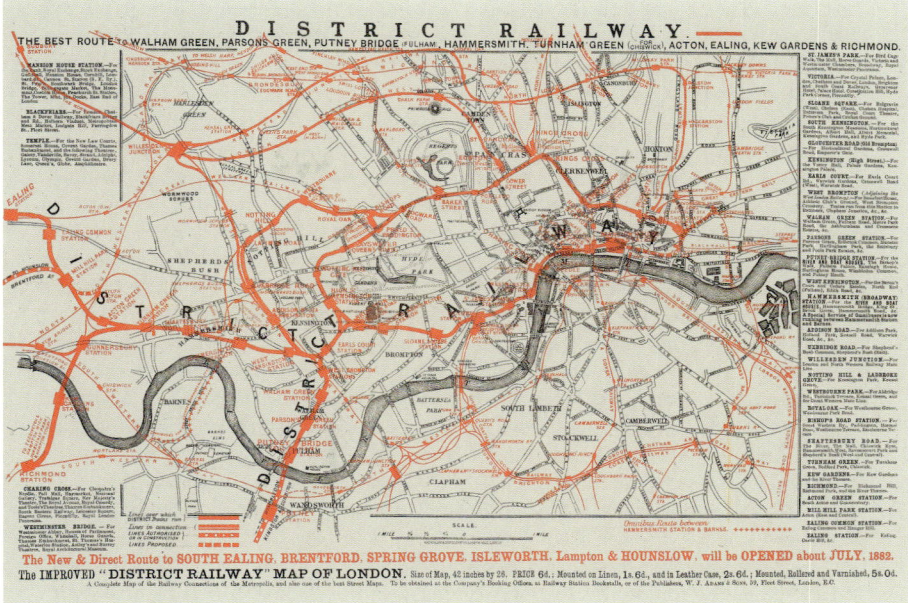

**The District Railway was a prolific producer of maps. This map dates from 1881 and is a 'Miniature' version sold at a halfpenny or folded into guidebooks.**

The District harboured thoughts of introducing lucrative freight business, but in the central area scope was very limited and facilitation of Midland freight traffic to Kensington was all that could be managed. When the Hounslow & Metropolitan, Ealing & South Harrow and Whitechapel & Bow railways were being planned the scope for goods traffic was investigated but not pursued, partly because the main line railways had already covered the areas with adequate facilities.

The District was more successful with parcels. From the 1880s both the Met and District successfully carried parcels, though the District did not carry unaccompanied parcels and newspapers continuously and there was a pause from about 1896. The service was fully restored in November 1902, though it only lasted until 18th March 1905, killed by impending electrification. The parcels were dealt with mainly at station booking offices, but where traffic was heavy parcels offices were provided with dedicated porters who conveyed them to and from the trains where they were carried in brake compartments with the guard. From stations it is recorded delivery boys using tricycles delivered parcels to customers.

An awkward commodity was fish, quantities of which the Billingsgate fishmongers insisted in sending by train from Monument for local distribution. Although much of this went early in the day, it was an especially obnoxious commodity that left highly unpleasant and slippery evidence behind. The District also carried mailbags, but usually they were dealt with by Post Office messengers at the stations and guarded by messengers on the trains. The District also carried unaccompanied luggage, in a similar manner to parcels. When the parcels service was withdrawn, conveyance of unaccompanied luggage was contracted out to firms such as Pickfords. Most stations at that time had attended left luggage offices so such a facility was straightforward, though stations would refuse livestock or items self evidently not classed as luggage. Left luggage facilities lasted until the 1960s, and although a few were replaced for a time by luggage lockers they are now only a memory.

When the District opened, the signalling and pointwork was operated mechanically from signal cabins generally located at each station or intermediate junction. Signals were 2-position semaphores, showing danger or caution (there was no clear position – operation in dark and smoke-filled tunnels was regarded an activity only to be undertaken with caution). Communication between signal boxes was made by means of electric telegraph instruments devised by C. E. Spagnioletti, the GWR's telegraph superintendent, and was essentially like that on the Metropolitan. From about 1880 the District superimposed Lock and Block apparatus based on the Sykes pattern. In effect it meant starting signal levers were electrically locked unless the correct sequence of operations by the signalman ahead, while passing the train in front, released the lock, making it nearly impossible to allow in error a train to enter a section already occupied. In later years a few signal boxes were introduced between stations to break up long sections and improve headways; these were all in tunnel, at Sion College, Elizabeth Street and Prince's Street and must have been dreadful places at which to work.

The District especially benefited from traffic to various London exhibitions. South Kensington station was near the Royal Horticultural Society (RHS) gardens, laid out in 1861 north of Cromwell Road, and used for holding large exhibitions. The first exhibition served by the station was the International Inventions Exhibition in 1871 to which from 1st May 1871 a connecting bus was run (jointly with the Met), though the operation was not apparently repeated. Exhibitions were held sporadically thereafter but became more frequent in the 1880s, in consequence of which a lengthy and expensive subway was built under Exhibition Road. It was the District's misfortune that these exhibitions died out within three years of the subway opening – the last being the Anglo-Danish in 1888, after which the grounds were built over.

Happily the District owned considerable land in the Earl's Court area, west of Warwick Road, and from 1887 this was made available to hold various annual exhibitions and 'spectaculars' which became a well-known feature. The first was the American Exhibition and Wild West show that opened on 9th May 1887 together with a covered way and new booking office from the west end of Earl's Court station (which for some years was only opened during exhibitions). A gigantic wheel came into use on 6th July 1895 and lasted ten years. It was demolished in 1906 and, worryingly, it was found in such poor condition that scrap contractor George Cohen had to repair it before it was safe to dismantle. The exhibition site was later expanded by bridging the West London Railway onto further District land to the west. A connection to the exhibition grounds was also made from the east end of West Kensington station. For the benefit of local residents who might find these direct connections useful special tickets were issued to allow passage in either direction through these two stations; the facility to buy such 'return toll' tickets at Earl's Court lasted a century. The District also installed its own ticket offices at many of these events; this was certainly done at the Anglo-Danish Exhibition in 1888.

The third source of exhibition revenue was from a new exhibition hall (called 'Olympia', the present Grand Hall) next to Addison Road station. This was built by the National Agricultural Company and opened on 27th December 1886 for the Hippodrome Circus. Here the District made revenue from the Middle and Outer Circle trains and through journeys from other District stations.

Wimbledon train at East Ham showing a mixture of 4- and 5-compartment carriages. This view (probably around 1904) shows the locomotive bearing a number of improvements made in the 1880s, including the conspicuous removal of the safety valve from the dome to the firebox.

Returning briefly to the South Kensington subway, both the District and the Met wanted to improve access to the RHS grounds, a quarter mile away. There were several proposals for achieving this but a simple subway finally won the day, becoming part of the joint station operation. Construction of this major work began in spring 1885 and the subway was opened commendably fast on 4th May 1885 (co-incidentally for another Inventions Exhibition). Intended only to open when exhibitions were on, a penny toll was charged; paid either at time of use or included in ticket prices. With the collapse of the large exhibitions in 1888 this expensive subway was thereafter rarely used until 1908 when it was opened free. The District obtained powers in 1906 to extend to the Albert Hall, but they were never exercised. From 29th September 1915 the subway was extended about 40ft at the northern end in connection with the construction of a new Science Museum building, into the façade of which a new entrance was constructed. The subway is still in service today, and while somewhat dreary provides a safe route between the station and the museums beneath the awkward and busy Cromwell Road junction.

To help bolster traffic the District operated feeder buses to several stations. In the 1870s and 80s several temporary bus services were run to major exhibitions or events at Chelsea (from Sloane Square) and Olympia (from West Kensington). From the late 1880s there were more conventional services. The first ran from Mansion House to Liverpool Street from June 1887 and was designed to short-circuit the roundabout CLER. From 2nd November 1889 a service began between Victoria and Upper Baker Street, extended to St John's Wood the following month; another route ran from Victoria to the Piccadilly end of Bond Street. These did not endure. A third route from the same date lasted much longer. This ran from Charing Cross to Upper Baker Street, weekdays only; it was advertised as running every 6–7 minutes and overall journey time was 26 minutes. Through tickets were issued from District stations, the singles of standard District pattern but overprinted with a triangle, and the returns divisible into three parts, the middle intended to be retained by the conductor on the return trip. Other significant feeder services ran from Putney Bridge station to Putney (Arab Boy) and from Hammersmith to Barnes (jointly with Met & Great Western). These services started on 5th July 1880 and provided a half-hour service on each route using just four buses. Connections were made into and from the District train service at Putney Bridge and Hammersmith, and through tickets were issued. By 1896 only the 'Arab Boy' service remained, running at 15-minute intervals on weekdays only for a penny fare. Returns, and through rail tickets, were no longer available. From maps this last route seems to have been withdrawn during 1901–2.

# Electrification

For thirty years the operation of the District changed in no important respect. The same locomotives hauled the same carriages in the same grimy conditions. This was utterly unsustainable – the District was seriously out of date and worn out, and public expectations were rising; in any case the technology made it impossible to increase services further. Electric railways, like the Central London whose construction began in 1895, seriously threatened to undermine traffic on the parallel District. Improving bus and tram services had already inflicted damage, requiring painful fares reductions. Something had to be done, but financially the District was in poor shape: existing shareholders had virtually given up hope of any dividend and raising money for new investment was going to be very difficult.

Electrification seemed essential. The Met was contemplating electrification for similar reasons and joint operation of the Inner Circle meant same traction system would need adopting. Although the Metropolitan had already conducted some experiments at Wembley in 1898 a larger scale trial was called for in view of the scale of the electrification scheme. The District and Met decided on a joint trial to test a 4-rail (ie twin conductor rail) direct current system and selected the section of track between Earl's Court and High Street Kensington which was not heavily used and where the effects of any mishap could be contained. The use of four rails rather than three was possibly due to the speed with which they could be laid, it being unnecessary to bond the existing running rails or risk interference with the telegraph circuits, neither being worth tackling for a mere experiment. The conductor rails were laid one on either side of the existing track, and at a slightly higher level.

A 6-coach train was ordered from Brown, Marshalls & Co to which was fitted electric traction equipment by Siemens, the two railways sharing the cost. The end vehicles were motor coaches equipped with driving cabs, and only the leading coach was under power in either direction. Electric power was supplied from temporary generating plant at the Warwick Road end of Earl's Court station.

Tests began in February 1900 with the train operating as required between Earl's Court and the District side of High Street Kensington. It entered passenger service on 21st May but the service was withdrawn from 6th November, the trials having evidently proved successful. A specification was then produced for full-scale electrification with significant speeding up of services and much improved headways. At this stage either a 3-rail or 4-rail system was considered equally suitable, but while it was obvious electricity could be utilised to great advantage there were various different systems available and neither party wished to prejudge the best equipment to adopt. Further investigation into the matter of electrification was undertaken by a joint committee of the two railways who went out to tender on a non-prescriptive basis and considered the responses in December 1900.

The two most plausible responses were investigated, one for a dc system (from Thomson Houston) operating at about 600 volts and the other for a 3,000 volt, 25-cycle three phase alternating current system (using twin overhead conductors) from Ganz of

Budapest. Both the District and the Met became convinced that the Ganz system was superior; certainly initial costs were lower and fewer substations were required (which could be unmanned). The proposal would have produced 6-coach trains with motor coaches at each end; these were to have been equipped with four 300hp motors apiece. After inspecting an experimental line in Budapest (in operation from December 1899) the companies came very close to complete acceptance of the tender, but the course of events was about to change.

As 1900 approached the District's finances were sinking badly and drastic measures were obviously necessary. An American traction financier, Charles Yerkes, became interested in the opportunity and with the New York stock exchange appearing more likely to supply fresh capital than London the upshot was that Yerkes and his advisers came across to London to investigate.

Yerkes, with District support, agreed to raise the necessary finance and on 15th July 1901 set up the Metropolitan District Electric Traction Company with a capital of one million pounds to finance and project-manage the entire electrification operation. An agreement with the District was swiftly concluded and Yerkes's interests soon obtained complete practical control of the District, Forbes departing soon afterwards. Yerkes was also interested in some dormant schemes for building tube railways in London and had already purchased the Charing Cross, Euston & Hampstead Railway in October 1900, and the Yerkes syndicate soon began to plan these various public works as a single operation.

One problem was that Yerkes's engineers had serious concerns about use of the largely untried Ganz system compared with the well-tested dc technology used in the US. A further visit to Hungary was made, during which Yerkes (irked to find the experimental line dismantled) became dissatisfied and refused to employ the system. The Met, uneasy about this sudden change in direction, decided to go to arbitration (half its costs being met by a desperate Ganz) but the outcome was a resounding win for the tried and tested dc system. Meanwhile, the Ganz system was deployed on the 67-mile and steeply graded Valtellina Railway in Italy from 4th September 1902 with such conspicuous success that it was soon widely replicated elsewhere on the Continent and the dc-orientated American General Electric Company enthusiastically promoted the system in the USA. This steeply graded, sharply curved and many-tunnelled line used equipment very similar to that proposed for the District but operating at 15 cycles rather than 25. Had the Valtellina line come into use a little sooner the Underground's electric traction system would probably have taken a radically different course.

The 4-rail direct current system that Yerkes agreed upon had been used in the USA and facilitated the installation of automatic signalling. Yerkes recognised that improved services could only be operated with electric trains and automatic signalling together. The District now decided to conduct large scale trials to understand how the electrification system, trains and signalling worked together. It may be recalled that the ESHR had not yet been opened (the District assumed full control from 1st July 1900), and this line offered a convenient opportunity to try out the new technology.

Two low voltage power rails were installed, one (outer) positive and one (centre) negative. A temporary power station (moved from Earl's Court) was erected near Alperton. The automatic signalling used track circuits and pneumatically controlled semaphores, almost identical to those in place on the Boston Elevated Electric Railway. Signal boxes remained only where there were points. Fourteen new electric cars were also delivered, and experiments began; success was to be anticipated – nearly all the equipment followed the latest American practice.

The District and Metropolitan's experimental electric train at Earl's Court (on eastbound local line), motor car nearest. The channel section current rails either side of the running rails are clearly shown. LT Museum

1903 stock set at South Harrow, motor car leading. The two prototype 7-car trains were built by Brush Electrical Engineering at Loughborough to essentially American design. Each train had three motor and four trailer cars. LT Museum

The cars were all open saloon cars of essentially American design built by Brush Electrical Engineering and were designed to operate as two 7-car trains. Three cars on each train were equipped with traction motors and driving positions; the end motors each had one fully equipped driving cab while the middle motors had gated ends (like the trailers) with a driving position at each end so that short trains could be run. One train was fitted with British Thomson-Houston control gear and the Christensen air brake, the other with control and air-braking systems by Westinghouse. Subsequently the BTH control system and the Westinghouse brake showed themselves as the more reliable and were adopted as standard. The two trains were subsequently much modified and rarely (if ever) operated in formations as long as seven cars.

The equipment all worked well and the District decided to open the ESHR line for the Royal Agricultural Show (at the Park Royal showground, between 23rd and 27th June 1903). There had not originally been intended a station between North Ealing and Perivale-Alperton (the 'Perivale' was dropped from 7th October 1910), but showground traffic made it worthwhile constructing one and an inextravagant wooden station was thrown up near Twyford Abbey Road, called Park Royal & Twyford Abbey. Unfortunately, treacherous weather caused embankment slips further north which threatened to delay the opening. The District decided to open to Park Royal only from 23rd June, running on a single line basis north of North Ealing to capture most of the promised traffic (though the show had only 65,000 visitors – fewer than hoped). On 28th June the whole line was opened as far as South Harrow, but services over the Met to Uxbridge had to wait a few more years. Park Royal had been intended as a temporary station but lasted nearly thirty years as the showground area developed as a major trading estate – the station was later rebuilt on a new site.

Although the District now had modernisation in its sights it is worth backtracking to an alternative proposal that left visible evidence in the form of a tube railway. In the 1890s train headways in the central area were constrained by the limitations of steam haulage together with the restrictive mechanical signalling systems. Journeys were also slow by comparison with emerging competition, such as the electric Central London Railway. One solution entertained by the District was to duplicate its tracks through the central area to provide an express electric service. The District deep level scheme, as it was known, took advantage of the District's freehold right of way between Earl's Court and Mansion House, providing a high-speed service serving only one intermediate station, at Charing Cross. The five-mile long line was at first seen as a stand-alone railway, but after a careful survey there seemed merit in extending it at the west end to rise to the surface east of Earl's Court (by the Knaresborough Place bridge); this provided better interchange, the opportunity of through running, and better access to depot facilities.

In 1897 (when deep level powers were obtained) a quite independent tube railway, the Brompton & Piccadilly Circus (BPCR), was established for a line from South Kensington to Piccadilly Circus; no physical connection was contemplated with the District or the deep level line. The BPCR was no threat to the District and was thought likely to help develop traffic as well as discouraging further tube schemes in the vicinity; to this end the District came to support it, taking over practical control in November 1898. From then the District became more interested in developing the new line than in duplicating its own, especially as electrification of the main system was now likely to address all of the District's mounting shortcomings.

In August 1899 the BPCR obtained powers to make a junction with the deep level line at South Kensington, as well as powers to build the deep level tube west of South

Kensington; it is evident the BPCR was taking priority. The BPCR was one of many tube schemes that lacked any means of funding but it is also one of those that came to Yerkes's notice through his interest in the District. His solution was to combine it with another unfunded tube (the Great Northern & Strand) to form the core of today's Piccadilly Line. The two tubes were amalgamated by an Act of November 1902. It was subsequently agreed to move the link at Earl's Court to a point west of West Kensington and widen the District as far as Hammersmith where the tube trains would terminate. When the new tube was constructed, junction tunnels and part of a length of platform were built at South Kensington for a future link with the deep level line, but with electrification in hand on the main line, the scheme was really all but dead.

Yerkes's Traction Company was designed to fund electrification of the District, but his interests now incorporated several tube railway schemes where economies could be achieved through simultaneous co-ordinated construction (for example in sharing the power station). For this the Traction Company was now inadequate and Yerkes therefore established the Underground Electric Railways Company of London Ltd (UERL) with a capital of five million pounds. By the District's Act of 1902 the Traction Company's responsibilities to electrify the District were switched to the UERL. Work could then begin.

The District was authorised to build its power station on one of three sites in the Walham Green and Parsons Green area, but the BPCR had a better site earmarked at Lots Road, by Chelsea Creek, and it was here that the great power house to serve all the UERL lines was built. Power house construction was amongst the earliest of the electrification works, together with the mile long cable subways to the west end of Earl's Court station. These works (begun in 1902) were complete by December 1904 with generation beginning in February 1905. The main power house building was 453ft long by 175ft broad and 140ft high; this contained the overhead coal bunker and 64 water tube boilers (on two floors) which vented through four chimneys. The adjacent turbine hall contained eight turbo-generators each producing 11kV at $33\frac{1}{3}$ cycles.

Electricity was conveyed at 11kV to Earl's Court station via the cable subway and thence via high voltage cables running along the tunnel walls or trackside cable posts to substations at Hounslow, Sudbury Town, Mill Hill Park, Kew Gardens, Ravenscourt Park, Wimbledon Park, Putney Bridge, Earl's Court, South Kensington, Victoria, Charing Cross, Mansion House, Whitechapel, Campbell Road and East Ham. Kew Gardens and Wimbledon Park were built and equipped by the District but owned and operated by the London & South Western Railway. Each substation was equipped with transformers and rotary converters that produced traction current at about 550 Volts. This was fed to the current rails through heavy duty cables such that each section of track between substations was normally fed from each end and each section on each track could be independently isolated.

Signalling was developed from that tested on the ESHR. Below ground there was rarely space to use semaphore signals and with the smoke they would have been difficult to see. Instead, moveable coloured aspects (still pneumatically operated) were installed at ground level in the space between the tracks; the lanterns were oil lighted at first, but were soon replaced by electric lamps.

At the main junctions power signalling was introduced, reducing the number of signal boxes at multiple junctions, like Cromwell Road. Power frames with fully interlocked miniature levers were installed and illuminated diagrams (the first at Mill Hill Park) indicated the position of trains. Points and signals were air-operated, with their lever-controlled electric circuits interlocked with appropriate track circuits. Some 410 track circuits and 488 signals were installed, with 13 electro-pneumatic signal frames in new or converted signal boxes. There were five additional boxes only intended for use in emergencies and 11 other boxes where mechanical frames and associated point-work had been retained but (as with the emergency boxes) the signal arms were converted for electro-pneumatic operation.

As signalmen could rarely see the trains they needed a means of identifying their destination prior to arrival, so they could set up the correct route. An ingenious electromechanical system was devised which passed an indication to each signal box of the destination of each train. It was but a small additional step to use these same data to provide passenger information by means of large indicators on the platforms. Most stations had a single indicator on each platform with the main destinations listed and against which a number 1 or 2 or 3 could be illuminated thereby denoting the destinations of the next three trains.

The District's steam-hauled rolling stock was incapable of adaptation to electric working and a new fleet was necessary, building on the experience of the ESH cars. Orders split between several car builders were placed in August 1903 for 420 cars – enough for 60 7-car trains. These were placed in England for 70 cars each from Brush Electrical Engineering Ltd of Loughborough and Metropolitan Amalgamated Railway Carriage & Wagon Co at Lancaster. The balance of 280 cars was ordered from a French syndicate led by Les Ateliers de Construction du Nord de la France. Sixty cars were made at their works in Blanc Misseron, but many (mainly trailers) were farmed out to other works in France at Ivry Port (Compagnie Français de Material de Chemin de Fer, 42 cars), Luneville (de Dietrich et Compagnie, 68 cars), Pantin (Desouches, David et Companie, 42 cars) and St Denis (Compagnie Generale de Construction, 68 cars). Wherever made, the cars were virtually identical to each other and were redolent of current American design.

**Train comprising 1905 stock at Ealing Broadway in 1908. Destination indicators (later moved beneath driver's window) were provided from the start, and the non stop 'target' from the inauguration of such working in 1907.** LT Museum

'Motor' cars equipped with traction equipment made up 192 of the cars; the rest were 'trailers' (or, briefly, 'trail' cars). The motors intended for the ends of complete trains had a single driving cab, while those designed to operate in the middle of trains had a cab at each end, so that three cars at either end could be taken off to leave a 4-car train in service. In fact only 48 of the 60 trains had this arrangement and the other 12 were to have had two 'middle' motors so that when uncoupled both portions could remain in service (the idea of splitting trains at Mill Hill Park with portions for South Harrow and Hounslow was entertained but not in fact introduced at that time). About half of the end motors had a luggage compartment behind the driving cabs but these were soon replaced with extra seating. The trailer bodies were built entirely of wood (which proved very troublesome later) but the motor cars had steel underframes to withstand the traction stresses.

Lillie Bridge Works was highly unsuitable for the new electric stock and was difficult to expand. The District purchased land west of Mill Hill Park station and laid out a series of car sheds and sidings suitable for the new electric fleet. Cars were delivered by rail directly to the new works and the electrical equipment, made by BTH, was then fitted and tested. Because Mill Hill Park was less suited to deal with service requirements on the eastern end of the railway, new sidings were also laid out in the triangle of land east of Earl's Court and at East Ham, together with new and rearranged sidings at Parsons Green. Part of the vacated space at Lillie Bridge was leased to the GNPBR for a tube railway depot.

The new trains were much modified during their life. To speed up loading at stations they were provided not only with enclosed end vestibules (open, gated platforms were more usual) but with centre doors as well. All doors were sliding and compressed air operated which was then revolutionary. A conductor on each car operated air valves controlling some doors on either adjacent car. The idea was ahead of its time and the system was cumbersome, unreliable and was removed; the doors became entirely hand operated by passengers but lacked any form of locking system. At about this time trains were fitted with 'wing' mirrors so the driver could look back along the train to see all was well, and this became a standard feature of hand-door stock. The axles and trucks were insufficiently robust and soon required major repair and strengthening, and within a few years very large numbers of trucks were replaced entirely.

The train formations proved inflexible, especially when the use of 7-car trains proved excessive. Between 1906 and 1910 some 34 trailers were fitted with driving positions at one or both ends: designated 'control trailers' these could lead in a 2- or 3-car train where only one motor was needed.

The first electric service was between Hounslow and South Acton and began on 13th June 1905. South Acton was at the end of the new but unused Acton Loop Line and had a single platform on the down line (next to the NSWJR station); a facing crossover north of the station allowed approaching trains to come alongside. Although for a few years both tracks continued northwards to a junction with the NSWJR line, no passenger trains ever used it, and little or no freight (though the Midland and the LNWR both obtained freight running powers). At the Hounslow end, the derelict Hounslow Town station far better served the town than any other and the District decided to reopen it. In order to keep serving the Barracks (and not wishing to operate two branches) an exceedingly sharp single-track curve was installed immediately north of Hounslow Town so that trains arriving from Acton could reverse and proceed to the Barracks, and vice versa. The entire section between Hounslow Town and Hounslow Barracks was single line, but traffic was not heavy.

The next electrified service was that between Ealing Broadway and Whitechapel, from 1st July 1905. The Met simultaneously attempted an electric service on the Inner Circle, but this faltered as the collector shoes on their stock kept slipping off and dislodging the current rails, causing huge delays (steam operation was resumed until the trains could be modified). Torrential rain also created flooding which caused havoc with the District service so it was not a propitious start. On 23rd July the Putney to High Street service was converted, followed by Richmond–Whitechapel on 1st August, Whitechapel–East Ham on 20th August and, finally, Putney Bridge–Wimbledon on 27th August, with through electric trains from Wimbledon to Whitechapel. In each case second-class bookings were withdrawn immediately prior to electric services starting. First class bookings were retained and the new trains each carried a first class car that differed little in appearance from third class except for better-upholstered seating. The noxious fish traffic from Monument was also banned from 13th May 1905, shortly before the smart new electric trains arrived. The ELR and the LTSR line east of East Ham, were not electrified and through services were withdrawn from July and September 1905 respectively.

The basic weekday off-peak service in 1907 was based on a range of overlaid services. A 15-minute service operated between Ealing Broadway and East Ham, while 30-minute services operated between Richmond and Mansion House, Wimbledon and Mansion House, Ealing Broadway and Whitechapel and Wimbledon to High Street Kensington. A 15-minute shuttle ran between Putney Bridge and Earl's Court, exten-

**Hounslow Town station occupied the site today used for Hounslow bus station. The elevated platforms provided for an extension to Whitton over a road bridge.** LT Museum

ded alternately to High Street Kensington. A 30-minute LNWR service ran between Willesden Junction and Mansion House via Addison Road, and the Inner Circle operated at 10-minute intervals. In all, 22 trains an hour ran between South Kensington and Mansion House, augmented during the rush hours to 27 trains. Fewer trains ran on Sundays. Most trains were either six or seven cars, with a few fives (in rush hours) and between two and four cars off peak. At this time journey times were not very different from steam days: Ealing to East Ham, for example, remained at about an hour and eight minutes. Journeys were later accelerated as experience was gained.

A 30-minute service ran between South Harrow and Mill Hill Park, while between Hounslow Barracks and Mill Hill Park intervals were 15 minutes, with alternate trains projected to South Acton. Services were augmented during rush hours, with some through trains to central London operated from Hounslow. These western branch trains were usually just two or three cars, though through trains were longer.

The LNWR service (an Outer Circle remnant) remained steam hauled until December 1905 when electric locomotives (provided by the District) took charge of trains between Earl's Court and Mansion House. The locomotives were built by the Metropolitan Amalgamated Carriage & Wagon Co and were quite similar to the passenger cars but much shorter (only 25ft) as they only needed to accommodate control equipment. This service was cut back entirely to Earl's Court in December 1908 after which the electric locos were redeployed.

A South Harrow train pulling away from Park Royal station; this station, only ever intended to be temporary, was replaced in 1931 by a new station further south.

Just before the First World War the LNWR decided to electrify its suburban lines including the Willesden–Earl's Court service, but the War caused some delays. The District had only electrified the Addison Road branch as far as the junction with the WLER, and although Addison Road itself was electrified (by the GWR to serve Hammersmith & City trains from Latimer Road) the LNWR had to supply everything else from its own new power station at Stonebridge Park. A temporary traction supply between Willesden and Earl's Court was complete from 1st May 1914 (Stonebridge Park came on stream on 21st February 1916) but unfortunately the LNWR's new rolling stock was incomplete. The District agreed to lend some of its 1913 'Gloucester' stock which had been delivered (but had not yet entered service) and this was used until 22nd November when the LNWR's own trains were introduced (some temporarily accommodated at Lillie Bridge as its Mitre Bridge depot was not quite ready). The electric service operated at 15-minute intervals and still reversed via Earl's Court east siding.

After modification, electric trains were infiltrated onto the Inner Circle workings from 13th September 1905 and by 24th September the whole service was electric and second class accommodation abolished. From March 1907 trains were reduced from six cars to five (four for a while, and at several other periods until the 1920s) and the District operated two trains in each direction, the balance being provided by the Metropolitan – the combined service operating at 10-minute intervals. The District paths were taken over by the Metropolitan from December 1907 but resumed from December 1908. The most profound change was an increase in frequency to 6 minutes from October 1908 and this lasted until 1926 when other arrangements were made as will be described. From 1916 to 1920 an additional District train operated on the clockwise service.

As mentioned previously the tracks east of Campbell Road belonged to the LTSR which had taken the view that widening was essential. Unfortunately this had not been completed when electrification works began and operations became complicated. The widening between Campbell Road and East Ham began at the latter point in February 1902 and was introduced piecemeal between April 1903 and August 1905 and included provision of conductor rails on the local lines only. The track formation was widened on one side or the other (or both) and resulted in four platforms being provided at all stations. In each case this comprised side platforms on the outer roads and an island between the centre (up slow / down fast) roads, except at West Ham which, being built new with widening already in mind, had two islands. The electrification equipment was provided and installed by the District at the LTSR's expense, but standard LTSR semaphore signalling was utilised.

Four tracking had not at first been contemplated beyond East Ham, but Barking (where the Tilbury and Upminster routes separated) was a more useful point and the works were extended there too, a major operation that included reconstruction of Barking station. Work was largely completed in July 1908. Two platforms were reserved for reversing electric trains (with sidings beyond), though two more were electrified in 1911. District electric trains were extended from East Ham to Barking on 1st April 1908 and the District's sidings at East Ham were enlarged and received additional running connections at the east end. As part of the electrification works some of the District's cars were transferred to LTSR ownership, but were always pooled with the rest of the District's stock.

While the electrification work was proceeding, the Underground Group's GNPBR was under construction. The new tube rose to the surface west of West Kensington station and ran parallel to the District as far as Hammersmith. The District's station at Hammersmith comprised an island platform on the south side, serving westbound trains, an eastbound platform, and two bay roads on the north side of the station. The District did not then need so many platforms and gave up the northern bay roads to allow dedicated platforms for the GNPB. Between Hammersmith and the new tunnels the railway was widened and GNPB tracks laid in on the north side. To the west of Gliddon Road bridge a new station called Barons Court was opened on 9th October 1905 with two rather narrow islands, one serving each railway.

The shifting of the District's maintenance facilities from Lillie Bridge to Mill Hill Park released space at the former sufficient for a new tube depot. An extremely long 6-road car shed was built along the eastern edge, each road stabling up to four trains. The GNPB trains had to negotiate a single line connection to the District (at the east end of West Kensington station) and run through the station before they could gain access to the GNPBR at the west end – all highly inconvenient. The remainder of the site at Lillie Bridge was retained by the District and converted into track and signalling workshops.

A new station between South Ealing and Boston Road opened on 16th April 1908 when the area showed signs of development. The station – first called Northfield [Ealing] – was soon renamed Northfields & Little Ealing, on 11th December 1911, while Boston Road became Boston Manor on the same day.

Once steam haulage had been abandoned the District's tunnel stations were all thoroughly cleaned and a lengthy programme begun of replacing wooden by concrete platforms. Now ventilation was less of an issue, over the succeeding thirty years many overall platform roofs were removed and some or all of the airspace covered over by lucrative property developments. The busier stations were necessarily subject to reconstruction schemes necessary to accommodate ever-increasing traffic. Both Victoria and Charing Cross, in particular, were rebuilt on several occasions. Many other stations were also improved and where possible the ticket halls were moved from street to basement level, often to link up with subway networks but also with an eye to releasing ground floor space for commercial use – the District remained heavily debt-ridden and the ordinary shareholders rarely received any return.

**10-car train at Whitechapel around 1909. This image appeared in 'Modern Marvels' (1910) where it was described at the longest electric train in the world. The train is just about to uncouple into two portions for onward travel west, where the platforms were too short.**

# The District in its Heyday

Some operational features soon proved unsatisfactory. Putney Bridge was the limit of District ownership and most of the High Street service reversed there by running south of the 2-track station to reverse on the running line, sometimes delaying the Wimbledon service. The District built an additional track around the back of the 'down' (southbound) platform and converted the former 'down' platform into a bay road, with hydraulic buffers at the south end. This was no easy job with the line on viaduct and the new bay road was confined to 6-car trains – though this was adequate for the High Street shuttles.

The layout at Mansion House was thoroughly objectionable with the bay roads either side of the through roads (so that any reversing move interrupted through services) and there was much redundant pointwork following withdrawal of steam operation. When the LNWR service was cut back (to Earl's Court) in 1908 the District reconstructed the entire south side of the station by removing the south siding and bay and widening the island platform considerably to fill the vacated space. The westbound line was rerouted to the southern face of the new island and the track alongside the northern face became a bay road, which, being between the running lines, avoided fouling movements. The work was substantially complete by May 1911.

Ealing Broadway was also a source of delay, bearing in mind cars were added and removed there and it handled trains entering or leaving service from Ealing Common depot. The answer was a third platform. This was constructed by lengthening the southern platform and installing a new face on the south side, creating a very long bay that stopped short of the train shed; it came into use from April 1913.

At Earl's Court the tracks through the two eastbound platforms converged immediately east of the station before throwing off the connection to the siding. This became a source of significant congestion and from 1914 a direct connection was put in between the local platform and the siding to alleviate the problem, which mainly helped reversing LNWR trains.

We left the District having reached the end of its ESHR property at South Harrow in 1903 but the rails (owned by the Metropolitan) carried on to Rayners Lane junction where they met the Metropolitan's 1904 Uxbridge branch from Harrow-on-the-Hill, the whole branch being electrified from 1st January 1905. At first the only stations were at Ruislip and at Uxbridge, though halts appeared at Ickenham (25th September 1905), Eastcote and Rayners Lane (both 26th May 1906) and Ruislip Manor (5th August 1912). Traffic developed slowly in this remote area but the District eventually felt it worthwhile striving for a service to Uxbridge and exercised its running powers from 1st March 1910, about one in three trains to South Harrow being projected westwards (providing an hourly off peak service).

The need to reverse Hounslow Barracks trains at Hounslow Town was highly inconvenient and from 2nd May 1909 the spur and the connecting curve were closed and the old direct line reopened. A new station (also called Hounslow Town) was opened on the direct line just east of the Kingsley Road bridge; at the same time the line between

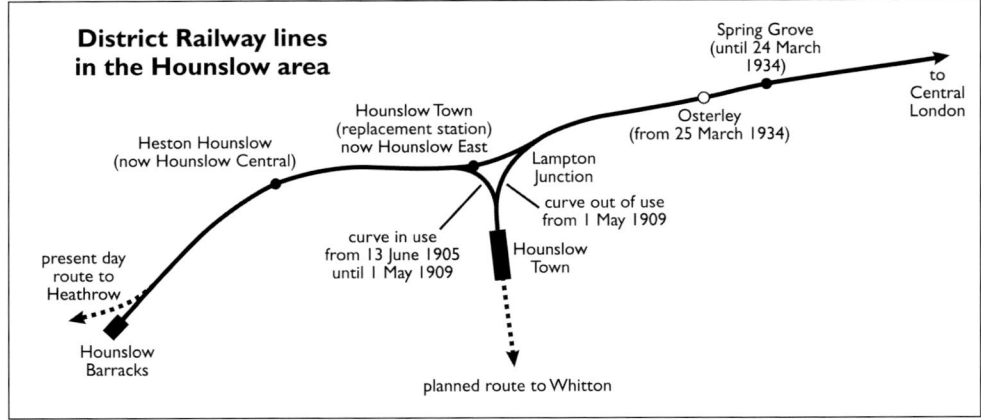

Lampton Junction and a point just short of Heston Hounslow was doubled. In 1912 Heston Hounslow itself was rebuilt as a double track station with island platform just east of its former site on the Lampton Road bridge, and the double line extended a quarter mile to the west. It wasn't until 1926 when the double line was finally extended all the way to the terminal station, which was rebuilt with three platform faces. By this time the station names had been simplified: Hounslow Barracks became Hounslow West, Heston Hounslow became Hounslow Central and Hounslow Town became Hounslow East, the changes being made from 1st December 1925.

At Mill Hill Park the convergence of branches and the need to reverse shuttle services from the west became a source of delay. It was decided to build a flyover just west of the station where the westbound Ealing line could cross the Hounslow branch, and to provide a three-track station (with two intervening island platforms) so shuttle trains would not foul main line trains. The work was completed during 1910 and the station was renamed Acton Town from 1st March.

Between Turnham Green and Ravenscourt Park the District's electric trains operated over manually-signalled LSWR tracks that still carried LSWR trains between Richmond and the West London Railway and Great Western trains between Richmond and Ladbroke Grove (the GWR having taken this service over from the Metropolitan when the Hammersmith & City was electrified); these trains became a source of delay to the District.

Agreement was reached to quadruple the line to provide a dedicated pair of tracks for the District's use. At Ravenscourt Park and Turnham Green the stations were adapted by providing separate island platforms on each company's tracks. A new station was built at Stamford Brook, with an island platform on the District tracks only. The new tracks came into use on 3rd December 1911 and the new station on 1st February 1912. The junctions at Turnham Green and Studland Road were removed and automatic signalling installed on the District tracks, which converged with the LSWR at Acton Lane; a junction was installed on the District tracks just west of Turnham Green where the Richmond line diverged from that to Ealing, the latter crossing the LSWR lines on a flyover. Although only used by the District, the electrified tracks remained LSWR property.

At the west end of Earl's Court the westbound Hammersmith and eastbound Putney lines crossed on the level, which was a source of delay. As there was plenty of

**Walham Green station, 1907. The station, rebuilt twice since this photograph, is today known as Fulham Broadway.** LT Museum

room and the District owned the land a flying junction was installed. The conflicting routes were shifted west and the eastbound line from Putney carried over the westbound to Hammersmith. The double track formations on the old routes were retained to provide a loop for westbound trains on the Putney line, while the eastbound line from Addison Road was carried to a point just outside Earl's Court before it joined the line from Hammersmith. The new works were introduced in stages, the last of which was commissioned in January 1914.

To take advantage of the connectivity between the LTSR and the Underground, the LTSR decided to operate some through trains. In 1912 the LTSR provided two sets of saloon coaches with central gangways, end sliding doors and retention lavatories that could operate along the District. A service actually started on 1st June 1910 (temporarily using standard LTSR coaches) which operated between Ealing Broadway and Southend or Shoeburyness. Trains were hauled as far as Barking by a pair of the District's electric locomotives (of which seven survived the withdrawal of the LNWR Mansion House trains) and changed there for LTSR steam locomotives. In 1915 there were three trains a day each way to and from Ealing Broadway. This curious service survived until wartime restrictions put paid to them on 30th September 1939.

At Whitechapel the northern platform was a bay road and when through services to the East London Railway were withdrawn in 1905 it was used to reverse diverted District and Metropolitan trains. Through Metropolitan services to the East London resumed in 1913 when that railway was electrified and the northern bay was then less heavily used and it was converted into a loop road by extending the track eastwards, bridging the ELR, and connecting into a siding that rejoined the main line; this substantial work came into use at the end of 1914.

Another development at Whitechapel was promoted by the LTSR who were troubled by frequent fogs that reduced capacity into Fenchurch Street and who wanted to be able to divert part of the service via a fog-free W&BR. Whitechapel platforms were already quite long but is was found possible to extend the westbound loop platform eastwards beyond the ELR bridge to a total length of 550 ft, long enough for 12-coach LTSR trains (though the extension was quite narrow). The existing south siding and a crossover at the extreme east end of the site allowed steam locomotives to run round and trains to proceed eastwards again. The arrangement came into use in May 1910 though it is unknown if it was ever used for the intended purpose. The extension survived until the ELR bridges were replaced in the 1950s.

From 1908 a 9-car District train operated from Barking to Whitechapel where it uncoupled into two portions for the rest of the journey; this increased passenger capacity at the busiest stations on the LTSR section while not increasing valuable train paths. This working was later increased to 10-cars (probably from when the platform extension was available). In 1912 there were multiple 12-car workings which uncoupled to produce 6-car trains, but by 1915 it was just one 10-car again, departing East Ham at 07.25; this train continued to uncouple at Whitechapel until 1925.

From the 16th December 1907 timetable so called 'non stop' working was introduced, though usually only a few stations were missed. East of Whitechapel in the morning there were at least twelve different non-stopping patterns. The simplest was the omission of one station, such as Mile End or West Ham, and the most complicated the omission of eight stations. By doing this it was possible for trains to depart from the most easterly stations regularly and gather together in bunches by Aldgate East, as the fastest caught up the slowest; this left a slight gap into which an Inner Circle train could slip from Aldgate. There was something similar further west in the evening when by judicious non-stopping west of South Kensington, gaps left by Inner Circles could be closed up, and services on the western branches evened out. Such complexity (with accompanying passenger confusion) is unlikely to have delivered the full theoretical benefits but clearly worked to an extent since from the 1920s non-stopping patterns were simplified and in that form carried on until as late as 1964.

Shortly after non-stopping was introduced 'non stop' boards were fitted to the front of trains (reading NON STOP or ALL STATIONS) and boards were fitted to the sides of cars listing the specific stations missed out. Later on train indicators on the platforms were rearranged to show non-stop trains together with the stations concerned. The Non-stop indicators consisted of panels on the outsides of trains alongside a number of doorways and were headed 'Not Stopping At', below which were mounted small swivelling plates, each with the name of one station on one side and blank on the other. A destination plate was also carried in a bracket at the top. Needless to say, changing all this paraphernalia at the end of each journey consumed much staff time; the fact the regulations needed to remind staff not to make the changes while the train was moving suggests short-cuts were not unknown.

That all doors were hand operated greatly eased the problem of changing the indicators on the offside at terminal stations, but correct door operation relied heavily on passenger compliance that was not always forthcoming. There was nothing to stop passengers pulling open doors on an accelerating train in order to leap on as a train started away, or to shut the door afterwards. Indeed in warm weather passengers would partly (or even fully) open doors to improve ventilation between stations.

Right **District Railway poster of 1909 promoting the new non-stop services to Hounslow.**

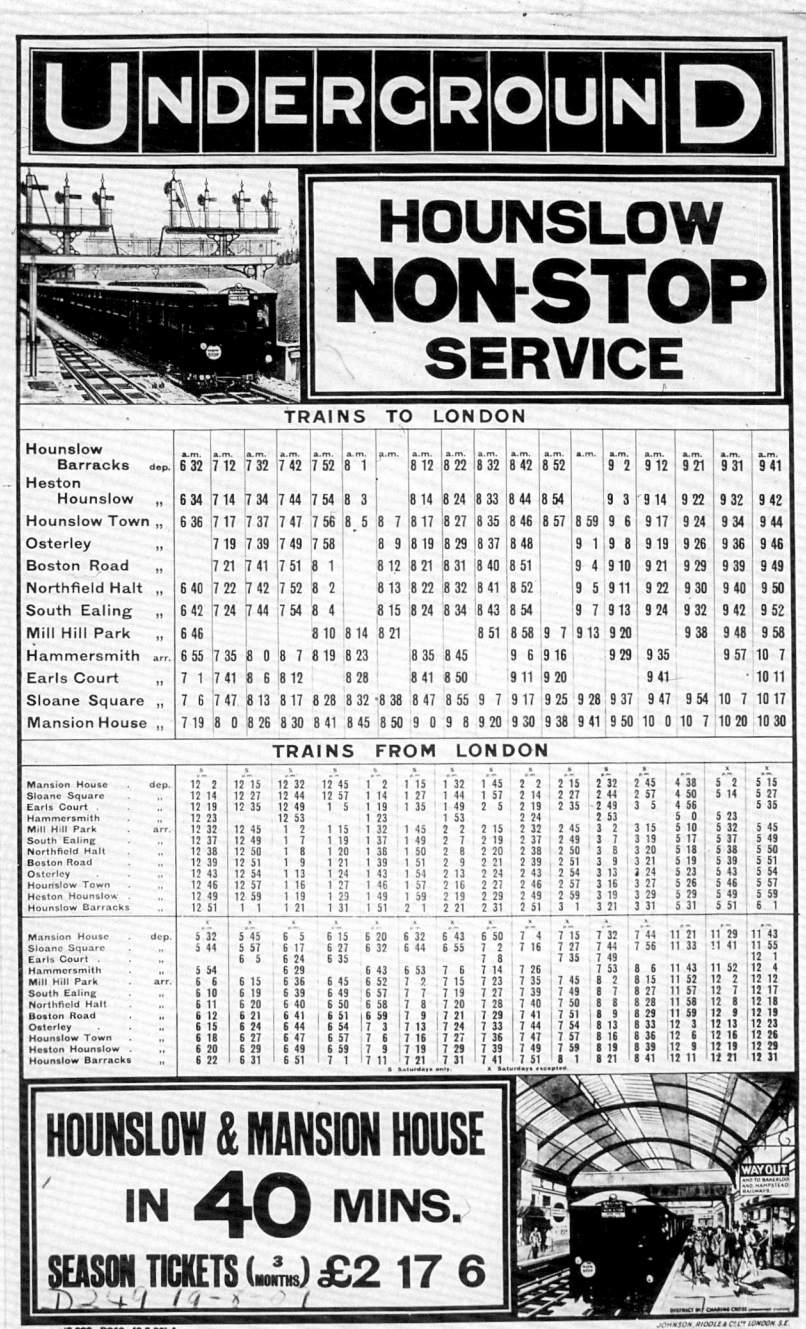

At Barking terminating trains stopped at an adjacent track to the through trains and (rather than embarking on the tedious route over the bridge) it was quite common to wait until a through train stopped, open the offside doors of each train and simply step from one to the other. In a desperate attempt to stop this dangerous practice, instructions were issued that through trains had to stop so that the doors did not line up. Although all the evidence suggests that there must have been accidents, they do not seem to have reached any level of prominence nor unduly influenced the District to return to power operation until the 1930s.

Peak hour electric trains on the main part of the District were at first 7-cars long, but many were soon reduced to 6 cars and both formations operated until December 1907 when 6 cars were the longest formation. After various experiments 8 cars were settled upon as a maximum and several were operating by 1915, increasing thereafter. The operation of 8-car trains was a mixed blessing as platforms (while of varying length) could rarely accommodate more than seven cars west of Whitechapel. At first it was determined that if the driver stopped accurately only the first and rearmost set of double doors would be outside platform limits, and passengers would get used to it. Certain stations (particularly in the open air) lent themselves to platform extension; in tunnel stations extension was sometimes possible but at first trains ran with the end doors locked. In due course narrow catwalks, about a half-car long, were installed at each end of the platforms into the tunnels, and staff had to be sure they were clear of any passengers before trains moved off. These remained in everyday use until the late 1970s. St James's Park and Charing Cross were two stations where platforms could be properly lengthened into spaces vacated by sidings not needed since steam traction was withdrawn. As mentioned already some 9-car trains were also tried, and in this case the rear car was only accessible at a very limited number of stations and a special attendant was carried to supervise matters.

By 1915 a small number of trains were scheduled to uncouple in service at Acton Town during the evening peak (midday peak on Saturdays), enabling through portions to serve the branches. This arrangement was later confined to 8-car 1920 stock trains which divided into a 5-car portion (leading) and a 3-car portion; one worked to Hounslow while the other worked variously to Ealing Broadway, Uxbridge or South Harrow (there was no corresponding eastbound arrangement). This facility endured until the Piccadilly Line extensions of 1932 rendered it unnecessary.

In the 1920s, in the height of the evening peak, 40 trains an hour were operating through the central area, mainly 6 or 8-cars, though Inner Circles were only 5-car. Even off-peak services were frequent, at 29 trains an hour in the afternoons, mainly 4-car, though Inner Circles were still five. Off peak services were based mainly on 10-minute intervals to Wimbledon and Ealing (and Putney to High Street) with a 15-minute service to Richmond and a 6-minute service on the Inner Circle, which combined to form a somewhat irregular cocktail of trains. The off-peak branch services were about 6–8 minutes to Hounslow (trains alternating to Acton Town and South Acton) and about ten minutes from South Harrow to Hammersmith, with alternate trains starting from Uxbridge. In the peaks there were several through trains from Hounslow and a single morning through train (composed of 8-car 1920 stock) from the Harrow branch, 'The Harrovian', that ran through from South Harrow at 08:13 and non-stopped Park Royal, Acton Town, Turnham Green, Stamford Brook, Ravenscourt Park, Barons Court, West Kensington, Earl's Court, Gloucester Road and South Kensington, in theory completing the South Harrow to Victoria journey in only 31 minutes; this train was operating as long previously as 1915.

To operate this intensity of service, slick operation required significant changes to the signalling. It was soon found that as train services and passenger volumes increased, the automatic signalling began to cause trains to bunch at the busier stations. The answer was to provide additional home signals (at least a second home and often a third). This allowed trains outside a station to move forward as soon as the train ahead began to move out of the platform. This move, coupled with other adjustments and the track works already referred to, allowed trains to move reasonably freely up to 40 trains an hour, and more precariously at even higher intensities. The ability to do this with trains with hand-operated sliding doors is little short of astonishing by today's standards, but the number of staff required to make it all work was significant.

The signalling east of Campbell Road was entirely mechanical in operation and became a significant constraint. The LTSR and its successor (from 1912) the Midland, endured the problem, but its successor from 1923, the London, Midland & Scottish Railway (LMSR), could not avoid action and it decided to install a 2-aspect colour light system between Campbell Road and Barking on the local lines only. Because of the large number of junctions, all signals were semi-automatic (with trainstops), under the overriding control of the existing signal boxes, though normally they operated automatically under track circuit control. The first section converted was Campbell Road to West Ham on 18th July 1927 and the whole project was complete by 1929.

The track and signalling improvements allowed more trains to operate but soon stretched the available rolling stock. In consequence, an order was placed in 1910 with Hurst Nelson for 32 motor cars and 20 trailers, with Metropolitan Amalgamated in 1912 for 22 motors and 8 trailers, and Gloucester in 1913 for 26 motors and 4 trailers. More motors were built than trailers to increase the proportion of motors from one in three cars to one in two, increasing train performance. The new cars were operationally interchangeable with the 1905 stock. The car bodies were mainly steel (though much wood was still used) and in appearance they were similar to the 1905 cars although those from Gloucester had elliptical roofs rather than clerestories.

**Metropolitan Amalgamated motor car shortly after delivery, coupled to a 1905 trailer with which it was visually very similar.** LT Museum

In 1920 the District took delivery of 100 new cars from the Metropolitan Carriage & Wagon Co. These could not be mixed with the existing pool and formed a class of stock in its own right. They were all-steel, with three sets of double doors per car side and were designed to operate in 8-car formations that uncoupled into 5-car and 3-car portions, the latter having a control trailer at its coupling end. Although there were to be only three motor cars on an 8-car train, each had all axles motored unlike earlier cars which had axles on only one truck motored, and in consequence the control equipments were duplicated. The trains were later found to be somewhat overpowered and the duplicate equipment and equivalent number of motors were removed from one motor car on each train. The original composition was 40 motor cars, 12 control trailers (first and third class composite), 12 first class trailers and 36 third class trailers, enough for 12 trains plus spare cars.

The original 1905 stock was indifferently made and the wooden trailers deteriorated quite rapidly and required considerable bodywork attention. The motor bodies were more robust, though trucks and axles were troublesome. By 1920 a number of these cars were in very poor condition and as it became possible to order new stock plans were made to scrap the worst wooden cars. Fifty new motor cars were ordered from Gloucester Wagon & Carriage Company; these were entirely compatible with the older stock. Each car had two sets of double doors per car side and compartments at each end, one arranged for the guard and one for the driver, with hinged doors for their exclusive use (on older stock these doorways could be used by passengers when not used by these staff). As with the standard cars on the District only one motor bogie was provided. When delivered in 1923, some forty-two 1905 motor cars were converted to trailers and equipped with new trucks; eight motor cars were also scrapped (including all six of the experimental 1903 cars). Meanwhile the remaining 1905 cars were reconditioned although by the end of 1924 some 26 trailers of 1905 origin had been scrapped, followed by nine more in 1925 and a further 14 in 1926. Some additional cars were out of use and a motor car had been lost in 1909 as a result of a collision. By the end of 1925 all 16 experimental 1903 cars had also been withdrawn.

Left **Metropolitan Amalgamated motor car taken in the 1920s. The interiors of the various batches were not greatly different.** LT Museum

Right **An eastbound District train pulling away from South Kensington in May 1925, with a 1905 car leading. The Metropolitan bay road may be seen on the right, and the platforms used by Circle trains on extreme right. This platform is used today for all westbound trains.**

In 1925 the Inner Circle service was run at 6-minute intervals with sixteen 5-car trains of which four were provided by the District on the anti-clockwise service. It was found in practice that the timings were too tight and the intervals too close, resulting in the service being prone to delay and unreliability. However this intensity of service was necessary on the High Street to Edgware Road section which was not served by any other line (though there were rare South Kensington–Aldgate trips).

From a traffic viewpoint High Street Kensington was not an ideal terminus as many passengers changed to the Inner Circle to travel further, particularly Paddington. In 1926 the Metropolitan completed a much-needed rearrangement of Edgware Road station as part of a plan for a new tube through north-west London to Kilburn, though this was not proceeded with. The rebuilt station had two island platforms with through and loop roads and could reverse part of the train service in either direction without fouling the main running lines. These new facilities offered an opportunity. The Inner Circle was recast at $7\frac{1}{2}$-minute intervals with a slightly more generous running time that required only 14 trains, all of which would now be provided by the Metropolitan. The District's contribution (it was jointly liable for operating the Inner Circle) was to extend its Putney–High Street service to Edgware Road and thereby improve overall frequencies along the busy western side of the Circle. On Sundays frequencies were reduced to 10 minutes and the District continued to provide four trains (two in each direction) partly to keep District crews familiar with the route.

At the west end of the District the widening between Studland Road and Turnham Green soon proved abortive. The GWR service between Richmond and Ladbroke Grove last ran on 31st December 1910 (before the works were even completed), and the LSWR service was soon reduced, then withdrawn altogether in 1916, following which the tracks became derelict.

The overloading of the District's western branches and heavy interchange with the Piccadilly at Hammersmith, coupled with the empty LSWR tracks west of Hammersmith, suggested the obvious solution of extending the Piccadilly Line westwards at comparatively low cost. Schemes were investigated from at least as early as

1912 and powers for a Piccadilly extension were obtained in 1914, but the First World War, inability to raise money and more pressing investment requirements meant nothing was done.

In 1922 the Underground's chairman (Lord Ashfield) stated publicly that he desired to serve Richmond, either by means of the Central London Railway (from Shepherd's Bush) or the Piccadilly via the LSWR tracks. Again, more pressing schemes took priority and all that was done was to renew powers in 1926, with additional authority to extend the duplicate tracks from Turnham Green to a point just west of Acton Town. By then housing developments in Ealing and beyond were demanding service improvements just as much as improved services to Richmond. At the same time an agreement was concluded with the Southern (successor to the LSWR) that gave operational control of the stations, signalling and tracks between Studland Road and Turnham Green to the District and LER, though the Southern remained responsible for the viaduct, bridges and earthworks, and for the remainder of the route from Gunnersbury.

Meanwhile pressure for improvement mounted. Residential growth of Heston & Isleworth Urban District (which included Hounslow) had risen by only 3,500 in the ten years from 1911 to 1921, but the following 10-year increase was approaching six times that. This welcome traffic increase had been partly stimulated by existing post-electrification service improvement (in steam days the service had been very unattractive), but without further modernisation capacity improvement was difficult. The South Harrow line was worse; not only was housing sparse but competing services ate into the little traffic there was. There was no incentive for the Metropolitan's Uxbridge line traffic to divert to the District's moth-eaten shuttle; South Harrow and Sudbury Hill competed with Metropolitan and LNER services, Alperton and Sudbury Town with the London, Midland & Scottish, while Park Royal and North Ealing vied with the Great Western.

By 1926 the emerging proposals foresaw four tracks between Hammersmith and Acton (and beyond) with fast and slow services on separate pairs of tracks, increasing capacity and speeding up services. The Piccadilly was to run a fast service on the inner pair of tracks, while the District served the outer pair. The proposed split of services on the western branches was not clarified until 1929, by which time the Piccadilly was to augment services to South Harrow and Hounslow but not necessarily to the entire exclusion of the District. The running of Piccadilly trains to Richmond had not been ruled out but in the interim it appears these trains would terminate at Turnham Green.

With the Piccadilly mopping up the increasing demand on the Hounslow and South Harrow lines, District capacity was freed up and services to all western branches were comprehensively rearranged. District services were concentrated on the Ealing, Hounslow, Richmond and Wimbledon outlets – with truncated shuttles from South Acton to Acton Town and from South Harrow to Uxbridge. Nevertheless, even as late as October 1930, it was proposed to run a few through District trains from London to South Harrow in rush hours. It was several years before planned service patterns settled down in reaction to frantic 1930s house building. By 1929 it had been decided to extend quadrupling as far as Northfields (to be reconstructed east of Northfield Avenue, making room for a new Piccadilly depot to the west); Piccadilly trains were to call only at Hammersmith, Turnham Green, Acton Town and Northfields, while the District would continue to provide an all-stations service. It was envisaged there would initially be a 2-minute fast Piccadilly service to Acton Town (where one in three trains would turn) leaving a 6-minute Piccadilly service on each of the two branches, augmented by the District.

Chiswick Park station during rebuilding. The eastbound platform has already been rebuilt but the original westbound platform is intact in the centre; this was replaced by the new platform on the right and the space used for the new Piccadilly Line westbound track. LT Museum

Financing modernisation and extension of the Piccadilly became practicable following the government's Development (Loan Guarantees and Grants) Act of 1929, one of the measures designed to reduce unemployment. Further construction powers were obtained in 1930 and work on the western extension began that December. One of the more difficult tasks was the need to alter track and signalling between West Kensington and Hammersmith to suit a west/west/east/east pattern (from two pairs of east/west flows) while two operational railways still ran a full service.

Between Hammersmith and Studland Road junction it was necessary to excavate a second covered way. This emerged at a point where the viaduct swung west, adjacent to the District Line tracks, and there was just room to squeeze one of the new tracks between them. What became the new District eastbound line had to be built just north of the viaduct until all the lines ran at the same level. This meant piercing the structure on the curve and the loss of five arches which (though disused) were replaced by a bridge. At Stamford Brook there had been only an island platform on the southernmost pair of lines, used exclusively by District trains. In future these would be the westbound District and Piccadilly tracks, so a new eastbound District platform had to be built alongside the northernmost track. No platform was needed for the non-stop Piccadilly trains.

Revised connections with the Richmond line were installed east and west of Turnham Green, including two eastbound goods loops for coal trains to West Kensington and High Street Kensington. The northern pair of tracks was projected westwards through Chiswick Park to Acton Town, requiring Chiswick Park station to be completely rebuilt with two side-platforms serving the District Line only. At Acton Town major reconstruction was required to convert the former three-track (with four platform faces) layout, to a five track layout, one of which was reserved for an isolated South Acton shuttle service (the line was singled from 14th February 1932 and the shuttle introduced the same day – for many years the usual service was provided by one of two special 1923 stock cars converted with a driving cab at each end).

The 4-tracking continued west to Northfields where a new, and resited, station was built, replacing the structure provided in 1908. This brought Northfields station much closer to South Ealing, whose closure was considered. Northfields was given a secondary entrance at the eastern end of its platforms, a long gallery linking the platforms with Weymouth Avenue, only 200 yards from South Ealing station entrance and less than 70 yards from the west end of South Ealing's platforms. Closure was dependent on two main factors, neither implemented: the opening of another station at Ascott Avenue, in the long stretch between Acton Town and South Ealing, and maintenance of an interchange with local buses, which Weymouth Avenue could not immediately offer. South Ealing's eastbound platform was given a contemporary awning and shelter in 1936 but continuing indecision resulted in it retaining the "temporary" wooden station ticket hall which had been erected while the widening work proceeded. It survived until 1989 when a pleasant modern station building and short westbound shelter were erected. The Weymouth Avenue entrance at Northfields was not to survive, being closed after traffic on 3rd May 1942, the concrete support structure remaining an intriguing sight even at the time of writing.

New signal boxes were built at Hammersmith, Acton Town and Northfields, with signal cabins elsewhere retained but modernised. Two-aspect coloured light signalling was installed where there were new signal boxes, but elsewhere a curious mixture of coloured light and electro-pneumatic semaphore signals was to be found. On the South Harrow branch the pioneering automatic signalling with semaphore arms was replaced by new coloured light signalling (commissioned between October and December 1932), but semaphores were retained at North Ealing and South Harrow for some years more. At the latter station a new crossover was installed to enable trains to reverse west to east in either platform, and five new stabling sidings were laid at the eastern end on land used many years earlier by the car sheds for the District's first electric stock. Between the stabling sidings and the eastbound line a reversing siding was added to facilitate turning around the shuttle service to and from Uxbridge.

Power supplies were also modernised. A new substation and control room was built at Alperton, which controlled further new substations at Sudbury Hill, North Ealing and Northfields. New substations also opened at Barons Court and Chiswick Park, the latter remotely controlling the existing District substation at Ravenscourt Park. The existing substations at Hounslow East and Acton Town were retained, but that at Sudbury Town was closed. Power was normally obtained from Lots Road.

The new works crept into use gradually. The first public indication was a notice that from 8th February 1932 certain local trains to Hounslow and South Harrow would no longer carry first class accommodation owing to the infiltration of Piccadilly tube stock onto the District's shuttle services so crews could be trained. Two weeks later first class accommodation was abandoned completely between North Ealing and South Harrow.

On 4th July 1932 the whole of the District service between Acton Town and South Harrow was withdrawn and replaced by through Piccadilly Line trains, one in three being extended westwards beyond Hammersmith. As part of these works a new depot was bought into use just west of the new station at Northfields; this then had space for a total of 304 cars and included a 19-road car shed and 2-track lifting shop. Some District trains used the depot freeing up some space at Ealing Common for a few Piccadilly Line trains. From the same date Piccadilly trains connected at South Harrow (rather inconveniently) with a continuing District shuttle between South Harrow and Uxbridge.

The platforms at Westminster in the mid-1920s after reconstruction, completed in 1923. The complicated arrangement of buildings above prevented an overall roof being built, and the platforms were given canopies that survived until the 1990s. LT Museum

The Warwick Road entrance to Earl's Court, as photographed in October 1927, led to a long gallery running along the top of the embankment before reaching a bridge at the west end of the platforms. LT Museum

Four-tracking was ready from Acton Town to Northfields on 18th December 1932, and from 9th January 1933 additional Piccadilly trains were projected beyond Hammersmith as far as Northfields, calling only at Acton Town. From 13th March, Piccadilly trains were projected to Hounslow West, with compensating reductions to District services in the peaks.

Off peak services on the Hounslow branch were a little eccentric. The through Piccadilly Line trains (as in peaks) did not call at South Ealing which was still regarded as a District Line station (like Ravenscourt Park), and public timetables instructed South Ealing passengers to catch a District Line train. During the off-peak the District had long since operated only a shuttle service to Acton Town and this arrangement was continued in an idiosyncratic way by using 2-car sets of Piccadilly stock, shown meticulously in the working timetables as District trains and ignored entirely in most passenger timetables. However at the extremes of the day these shuttles continued to comprise District stock. This arrangement continued until 29th April 1935 when an enhanced off-peak Piccadilly through service from central London saw off the shuttles. As these were the only off peak trains they had to call at South Ealing (which was still, unhelpfully, District-only in peaks); peak Piccadilly trains began to call from May 1942, following closure of the Weymouth Avenue entrance at Northfields.

Several District Line stations were rebuilt during this period, the designs influenced by Charles Holden's architectural practice – several buildings are now listed. In particular Northfields (1933), Ealing Common (1931), Acton Town (1932), Chiswick Park (1932) and Hammersmith (1932) were all totally rebuilt. Hammersmith retained only its 1906 facade onto the Broadway, but a new facade was built facing Queen Caroline Street (though a modern development has swept all this away). Hounslow West (1931) and Boston Manor (1934) were rebuilt only at ticket hall level, and Stamford Brook gained a new eastbound platform in the new style, but the existing island was left alone.

**New station building at Chiswick Park under construction in 1932.** LT Museum

The old Osterley & Spring Grove station was closed, replaced by a new Holden station on The Great West Road. The former station building in Thornbury Road, closed after 24th March 1934, was for many years a bookshop; some thought was given to providing a footpath to the new station but the cost was not felt justified. At Hammersmith, Acton Town, Ealing Common and along the Hounslow branch, platforms were altered to 'compromise' height, half way between the car floor levels of tube and surface stock, giving a rather high step up into District Line trains. Holden began his association with the Underground at the District's Westminster station when, in 1924, the tiny secondary exit to the Embankment was updated and rendered to look like stone set in a rather geometric style that was later to be replicated elsewhere in granite or Portland stone. St James's Park station benefited from the construction above of the Underground's headquarters building at the confluence of Broadway with Tothill Street into which the eastern ticket hall was incorporated, the work being completed in 1929.

The simplification of the District's western branches was counterbalanced by further projection to the east. The LTSR had not been able to afford to electrify beyond Barking although the services were intensive and lent themselves to electric operation. When the Midland took over in 1912 it was an express condition of Parliament that the whole railway be electrified. Little was done before the First World War (which arrested the progress of many railway schemes) and matters were reviewed immediately afterwards. There were high expectations of something being done quickly, even to the extent of the District's 1920 stock being fitted with non-stop indicators for stations east of Barking. The Midland was optimistic about proceeding and encouraged the London County Council to look at the area west of Dagenham to build a vast new housing estate, ultimately housing 100,000 people. The Becontree Estate, built on either side of the railway, began to be occupied from 1921, though most of it came into use in 1925 and 1926; it lacked a convenient station until Gale Street opened on 28th June 1926, partly fulfilling the need.

The LMSR, which inherited the Midland in 1923, was in no better a position to electrify the whole of the LTSR line but it was obvious that west of Upminster existing and potential developments required service improvements. In 1929 the LMSR proposed to quadruple the line from Barking to Upminster and electrify one pair of roads – there was a reasonable business case but it asked for release from its 1912 obligation to electrify the whole of the LTSR, and Parliament acceded.

The LMSR did not propose to electrify its own service at this stage and trains were to be provided by the District. The new electric tracks were available for trial running from 4th September 1932 and the new passenger services were introduced on 12th September. The existing stations at Dagenham, Hornchurch and Upminster were adapted for four platforms, and Gale Street was completely rebuilt as a four-platform station, acquiring the name Becontree from 18th July 1932. New stations serving the electric lines only were opened at Upney and Heathway (better sited for the LCC estate) when the new lines came into use. Upminster Bridge was added from 17th December 1934 and Elm Park from 13th May 1935, again serving only the electric lines, and these were built to satisfy demand from new building estates totalling 10,000 people. Trains from Upminster initially operated at about 8-minute intervals in the peak hour and 20 minutes off-peak. During the rush hours LMSR trains often called at Upminster or Hornchurch or Becontree or Dagenham or Barking, but rarely more than one because of the limited track capacity. Early, late and off-peak trains stopped at more of the foregoing stations, and some at all of them, including East Ham, but not stations further west until Burdett Road.

Power for the new extension was obtained by the LMSR from the County of London's supply at Barking and then fed to new substations at Upney, Heathway, Hornchurch and Upminster; a control room for the new plant was built at Heathway and the other substations were unmanned.

Single-lens searchlight signals were introduced that could show one of three aspects (red, yellow or green) depending on track conditions. When the red or yellow aspect was shown an additional red marker light (mounted underneath the main lamp) was illuminated. In the event of a signal remaining at danger whilst working entirely automatically the marker light would go out after one minute and a yellow calling on light would illuminate to authorise an electric train to proceed with great caution. A somewhat similar system was also installed by the LMSR immediately afterwards between Euston and Watford, shared with Bakerloo Line trains. Trainstops were provided at all signals.

At Barking few track alterations were required. The arrangement there was a pair of tracks on the south side for the fast services, a pair on the north side for local and Tottenham & Hampstead services, and a pair of bay roads (platforms 4 and 5) in the centre of the station for electric services. On the extreme flanks of the station were up and down loop platforms, making eight in all. When electric trains were projected eastwards all that was necessary was to electrify the local platforms (2 and 3) and put in the connections to the new tracks about quarter of a mile to the east; terminating electric trains still used the bay roads. At Upminster three platforms were electrified, both faces of the island on the north side and the north face of the next island. The most northerly platform was also used for Romford–Upminster service, though the branch had access to all three platforms. East of the station was an electrified traffic siding as well as a single-track link to six electric stabling sidings some way beyond; these were intended for District trains to stable, reducing dead mileage to and from East Ham.

**In 1932 the District extended to Upminster over a widened and electrified LMS railway, and this view shows a District train at about that time. The second car shows well-filled first class accommodation and the leading car shows the casual approach to closing the manual doors in warm weather.** LT Museum

In 1926 the District introduced a classification scheme which made it easier to refer to the confusing array of trains it now operated; this proved extremely convenient and was later expanded by London Transport.

- B   Unrebuilt cars of 1905 origin (nominally 329 cars, but many unusable)
- C   1910 Hurst Nelson cars (52 cars)
- D   1912 Metropolitan Amalgamated cars (30 cars)
- E   1913/14 cars from Gloucester (30 cars)
- F   1920 Metropolitan Cammell (incompatible with other cars) (100 cars)
- G   1923 cars from Gloucester (50 cars)
- H   Rebuilt 1905 cars (42 cars).

The above totalled 633 cars, of which 526 were required for the evening peak service of 86 trains, which included one traffic spare. Nevertheless the rolling stock was under pressure from demand for service improvement and the rapid deterioration of the 1905 cars.

A review in 1926 produced a major reorganisation involving considerable modification to existing cars, the purchasing of new cars and the further withdrawal of 1905 stock. The F stock (40 motors and 60 trailers) remained largely unchanged by this programme as it was fairly new and incompatible with anything else.

The remaining stock was broadly divided into two types. The first was intended for the main section of the District and was equipped with BTH control equipment. This comprised 263 motors made up of 52 C, 30 D, 30 E, 50 G and 101 new motor cars designated class K. With these would operate 248 trailers (the vast majority of 1905 origin). The second type of stock, with older traction equipment, was intended for local services on the western and High Street branches and would comprise 37 motor cars and 18 control trailers, all of 1905 origin. This totalled 566 cars (666 cars including F stock).

With 101 new cars (but an increase in fleet size of only 36 cars) there was considerable scope for culling the worst of the B stock, and a further 67 trailers had been scrapped by the end of 1929; in addition a further 110 B stock motor cars were given a new lease of life and rebuilt as H stock trailers (making 152 in all). Ninety-six unrebuilt (but fair condition) B stock trailers survived. This net reduction in motor cars was partly redressed by the conversion of all 32 C, D and E trailer cars to motors (contemplated in their design).

A feature in all this was considerable rearrangement of the electrical control equipment, including the positioning of the air and control lines from the centre of the car ends (under the coupler and above the communicating doors) to the sides of the cars. This loss of symmetry meant that it was no longer possible for cars to couple either way round, as the air lines, auxiliary and control circuits could no longer be physically connected if a car was 'turned'. This complication (known as handing), meant that motor cars had for the first time to be designated 'east-facing' or 'west-facing' and modified in the correct numbers to produce the standard train formations required. Previously any imbalance in cars caused by accident, overhaul or heavy maintenance could be corrected by turning odd motor cars via the Cromwell Curve triangle, but now cars could only be turned in conjunction with major workshop attention. The decision was made in the case of the main-line stock to create a basic set of 4-cars (with an east- and a west-facing motor car and two trailers), and a number of 2-car sets with an east-facing motor car and a single trailer. The 2-car sets would not operate as trains in their own right, but one or two could be added to the east end of a 4-car set to create 6-car or 8-car trains as required. All trains would thence be of 4, 6 or 8 cars. This modification

A typical off-peak scene at Earl's Court in April 1931. A 4-car Hounslow West train (G class leading) enters the westbound main platform with what is probably a Putney train in the westbound local. The Olympia sign indicates that trains then went from the main platform as it was the one most conveniently accessible from the siding; today they come from High Street and depart from the local platform. The use of 'Olympia' refers to the exhibition halls as the station was then still called Addison Road. LT Museum

work was substantially complete by 1930. The timetable of that year required an 89-train service (575 cars) comprising 27 x 8-car, 48 x 6-car, with 1 x 7-car and 1 x 5-car (both F stock) trains on the main line service, 2 x 5-car, 4 x 4-cars and 1 x 3-car on the local services, 1 x 6-car traffic spare train and 4 x 6-cars on the Putney–Edgware Road service (six trains in all) that were composed of 2 x 3-car sets of local stock.

The new K stock cars (all motors) were of broadly similar pattern to the G stock, but of smoother external design and with less ornate interiors; all cars were built by the Birmingham Railway Carriage & Wagon Co. The guard's position was more closely integrated with the passenger saloon, but still had hinged doors that could not be used by passengers.

Additional cars for the Upminster extension were partly obtained by release of cars from the western extensions and partly by 45 new vehicles ordered from the Union Construction Company (though Metro Cammell built the bogies). The new cars were designated L stock and were similar to the K stock (but lighter) and the design was adapted to incorporate trailer cars (37) as well as motors (8). Each trailer had sliding doors at the car ends in addition to two sets of double doors per car side, and this time the guard's door on the motor cars were sliding too, so they could be used by passengers. The excess of trailers portended a further culling of B stock wooden trailers.

During the 1920s the Underground Group consolidated rolling stock major overhaul all in one place, allowing each line's depots to undertake routine maintenance only. A substantial overhaul works was constructed on land south east of Acton Town and every 3–4 years cars were completely stripped down, equipment overhauled and bodies repainted. It was some years before stock from all lines used the works, which was progressively expanded to reach its largest extent after the Second World War.

# The London Passenger Transport Board

In July 1933 the UERL, Metropolitan Railway and a number of other transport undertakings were absorbed by the London Passenger Transport Board (LPTB), a new public corporation. The District Railway, as a UERL subsidiary, was absorbed into the new organisation and was henceforth promoted as the LPTB's District Line.

An early result of this amalgamation of interests was the working of Piccadilly Line trains beyond South Harrow. In contrast to earlier suggestions that the Piccadilly should be projected only to an improved Rayners Lane interchange station, it was now felt that the rapidly developing suburbs demanded through trains all the way to Uxbridge. It was first necessary to adjust Met platform heights to suit both tube and surface stock; when complete, a through Piccadilly service to Uxbridge replaced the District's South Harrow–Uxbridge shuttle from 23rd October 1933.

Another benefit quickly championed by the LPTB was a link from the west end of the platforms at Monument to the south end of the platforms at Bank on what was later called the Northern Line; this involved a long passage and a deep flight of escalators, which came into use on 18th September 1933, completing plans developed by the former Underground Group. Interchange from the District to the Central London Railway was also possible by walking the full length of the Northern platforms and an equally long and dreary subway. Curiously, Monument continued to enjoy a separate name although name boards were altered to 'Monument for Bank' or 'Bank for Monument'.

In December 1934 the LPTB and LMSR concluded a joint investigation into traffic on the Barking Line, already heavily overloaded and with developments further east threatening to make matters worse. The main constraint was the crossing of the District and the Met services on the flat (west of Aldgate East and east of St Mary's, as Met trains still ran onto the ELR). A commendable 36 trains an hour were operated in each direction along this short section of line, despite the two junctions; of these, 27 were District and nine were Met trains to and from the ELR. This bottleneck required five District Line trains to be turned east to west at Mansion House in the evening peak, maintaining District services further west at the required capacity but not doing anything for the overcrowded trains east of Cannon Street.

Analysis showed that most Met passengers continued along the Whitechapel route rather than to ELR destinations; indeed their need to change trains at Aldgate East was contributing to delay and overcrowding. The answer was to switch at least some of the Met trains towards Barking, which would increase capacity through the bottleneck to 39 trains an hour by reducing conflicting junction working at St Mary's and passenger delays at Aldgate East. The Southern Railway (which had an interest in the ELR) did not want all the Met trains withdrawn without testing the result, so it was proposed to maintain four trains an hour to the ELR and run eight through to Barking, which would allow Barking line services to be increased, in theory, from 27 to 35 trains an hour. As part of this scheme, improved interchange at Whitechapel would be made between the District and ELR platforms where ELR local services would be improved to make up the loss of through trains.

The District was renowned for its ability to move parties of schoolchildren and others for days out in what were then the country districts. Parties of 3000 or so were not unheard of, shifted in either direction by several special trains and special staff. LT continued the facility for some years and this view, at Ravenscourt Park on 30th July 1934, shows a party of 80 adults and 1500 children entraining a special for Eastcote (by then not usually served by the District). LT Museum

An eastbound Barking train approaches the junction with the little-used 'Cromwell Curve' in May 1935, G stock car leading. On the right are some District car sheds (the Metropolitan tracks are further right, out of view). In the distance is Cromwell Road signal box (closed the following month), with its panoramic view. LT Museum

A preliminary service began on 30th March 1936 comprising a morning working from Hammersmith (Met) to East Ham and back, and an evening trip from Hammersmith (Met) to Plaistow and back. The new timetable proper came into use from 4th May 1936 with eight 6-car trains an hour scheduled between Hammersmith (Met) and Barking during rush hours, and District services recast to accommodate them. Off peak, the Met trains reversed at Whitechapel.

The much-increased service to Barking required some track alterations there. Platforms 2 and 3 were used for through electric services and platforms 4 and 5 were bay roads, with lay-by sidings beyond. To make the layout more flexible a new up loop was provided through platform 5, so either platform 3 or 5 could be used for up local services as traffic required. This left platform 4 to accommodate reversing trains without fouling movements in the other direction. Various other track and signal improvements were made at the same time. In the peaks several District trains were extended from Barking to Dagenham where from 24th November 1935 a new electrified bay road and a stabling siding had been installed on the down side. Also part of the scheme was improved signalling in the Aldgate East area and a substation at Tower Hill.

These improvements were soon found to be quite insufficient and the track layout at Aldgate East was the main culprit. As part of a scheme of new works undertaken jointly with the main line railways it was decided to rebuild Aldgate East station on a new site about a train's length to the east of the old site. This released space into which the eastern arm of the triangular junction could be extended so that 8-car trains could stand on any part of the triangular junction without the rear end fouling the path of a train proceeding along another route.

**The new platforms and station at Aldgate East came into use in 1938. This view looks east away from the junction between the District and Hammersmith & City lines.**
LT Museum

67

The works were immensely complicated as the track through the new station site had to be lowered significantly to provide headroom for the new roof beams. The new station was opened on 31st October 1938 and in the following four weeks the old platforms were removed and the new tracks, junction work and signalling laid in; the entire southern curve linking Aldgate East and Minories Junction had to be replaced by a new tunnel slightly to the south (a substation was later built in the old one). The new junctions and signalling were commissioned on 27th November. When all was complete the new station had platforms more than sufficient for 8-car trains and entrances at either end, the western entrance not being far away from the old station. The wide platforms also had plenty of space to accommodate people changing trains. St Mary's station was partly superseded by the eastern entrance to the new station and was closed after traffic on 30th April 1938.

To improve capacity further it was decided to put more Met trains on the Barking line. From 8th May 1938 some further trains from the Hammersmith & City section were switched from the ELR to East Ham, increasing that line's contribution from eight to ten an hour. From 17th July 1939 the Metropolitan's Uxbridge service supplied eight 8-car trains an hour during the peaks to Barking from the north side of the Circle; this was an ingenious way of providing 8-car trains, as Hammersmith & City trains were restricted to 6 cars by platforms west of Baker Street – these now served either Aldgate or the ELR. The new pattern was complicated to operate, transferred delays between lines and was dogged with misfortune. There were at first insufficient 8-car trains to operate it, and a number of 6-car Q stock trains were borrowed to get it going. The Battle of Britain bombing of the City, which shut down the north side of the Circle for many weeks in late 1940, hardly helped promote the new service either. It was finally "suspended" from 6th October 1941 with all the Met's Barking trains sourced from the Hammersmith & City Line. This time the entire peak service was projected onto the Barking line and the through

> ## PROTEST OVER DISTRICT RAILWAY SEATING RULE
>
> *If third-class carriages on the District Railway are full, passengers with third-class tickets are allowed to sit in a first-class carriage if they are east of Charing Cross.*
>
> *West of Charing Cross they are permitted to stand in the first-class coaches, but not sit.*
>
> THIS strange rule of London Transport, confirmed to-day by an official, is to be the subject of a protest on behalf of Wimbledon passengers.
>
> A former Mayor of Wimbledon may stage a "come-back" after ten years, in order to fight for the second time what he describes as "the appalling overcrowding" on the branch to Wimbledon.
>
> He is Mr. T. G. Hatherill-Mynott, Mayor of Wimbledon 1925-26.
>
> Some time ago he wrote to the present Mayor of Wimbledon, Alderman E. J. Mullins, pointing out the inadequacy of trains, and the unfairness to Wimbledon passengers, who are unable to sit in first-class coaches if the third-class are full.
>
> He asked if the Railway Facilities Committee—a committee of the council—still functioned, and if it did, would they not do something to help the health of the Wimbledon residents?
>
> Mr. Hatherill-Mynott is himself a daily traveller on the line.
>
> ### "INTOLERABLE."
>
> "Things are worse now than they were 20 years ago," he said to-day. "More people are travelling to and from the City every day and things are becoming intolerable."

**The provision of First Class facilities was irksome on crowded trains and London Transport contrived some complicated rules to ease the pain. Non First Class accommodation was officially denoted Third Class at that time, following main line practice (Second Class officially existed on certain trains).**

trains to the ELR ceased for good, not only improving capacity along the main flow but avoiding an irritating conflicting movement that was a source of delay. The 1942 timetable shows 30 trains an hour running east of Whitechapel, nine from the Hammersmith & City to Barking, 16 District to Dagenham or Upminster and the balance of Districts to East Ham or Barking.

To operate the Met's Barking line contribution four more trains (plus spare cars) were needed to supplement its existing stock of 1904/5 origin. For convenience, the LPTB opted to purchase similar cars to the 'L' stock: 28 new cars, designated 'M' stock, were purchased from the Birmingham Railway Carriage & Wagon Co, half motors and half trailers, and were made up into the usual 4+2 formation (these trains ran as 4-car sets off peak). They were equipped with electro-pneumatic brakes and two sets were equipped with air-operated doors, both being novel features on the sub-surface lines at that time. The guard would usually release the doors and had responsibility for closing them, but once released each door set could be opened individually by passengers operating a locally situated push button. The system was called 'passenger door control' and its future development was to hinge upon the success of these trains.

In addition to the 'M' stock the LPTB also wanted to continue replacing the remaining 78 B stock trailers, which were deteriorating rapidly. This was achieved by purchasing a further 26 trailers (known as 'N' stock) from Metropolitan Cammell, again of similar design to the earlier L stock; as these had to be compatible with other District trains they lacked electro-pneumatic brakes and air doors.

The above measures were a stopgap as the District's 1905 cars were at the end of their useful lives and in rapidly deteriorating condition. The LPTB wanted to introduce trains composed entirely of motor cars equipped with 'Metadyne' control equipment, which would significantly increase rates of acceleration, allow regenerative braking and significantly reduce overall energy requirements. This was straightforward on parts of the Metropolitan Line as whole trains needed replacement and they accordingly received cars of 'O' stock (on the Hammersmith & City section) and the similar 'P' stock (on the Uxbridge service).

The District was an entirely different proposition as many cars were less than 15 years old, and only the trailers and a few motor cars really required replacement. This mix made it difficult to introduce complete new train sets, nor could they operate to their full potential with so much old stock still in operation. The forward-looking solution was to build a large number of new trailers to the new design but capable of conversion to motor cars at some future date. In the meantime they would be delivered with equipment entirely compatible with the existing District fleet with which cars they would be interchangeable.

Known as Q stock, 25 new motors cars and 183 new trailers were therefore ordered from Gloucester Railway Carriage & Wagon Co. All cars were flair-sided and had elliptical roofs and were quite unlike any previous cars on the District, though similar to the new Met cars. Each had two pairs of double doors along each car side and a single doorway at one end; at the other end was a hinged cab door which provided entry to the driving cab on motor cars but was sealed shut on the trailers, the interior space being used for extra seating. All cars had 600 volt power bus lines and auxiliary equipment, and the motor cars had the District's standard BTH control equipment. The motor cars and 58 of the trailers were designated third class, while 125 trailers were composite first/third, and had a partition separating the two sections. It was intended to scrap all the rotting 1905 stock but the Second World War caused some to have their lives extended, with three remaining in service until 1948.

Prior to Q stock arrival, there were 112 cars of C, D and E class, all motor cars. These were retained to provide a self-contained pool of five 8-car and sixteen 6-car trains. To balance car types, 14 C stock cars were converted to trailers (including eight control trailers) and 37 L, 26 N, and 14 M stock trailers were contributed, the latter transferred from Hammersmith & City Line. This pool (referred to as H stock) retained hand-operated doors, were not equipped with electro-pneumatic brakes and was also intended to contribute six 4-car trains for use on the ELR and two 2-car trains for the Addison Road–Edgware Road shuttle.

The new Q stock cars were delivered equipped with air-operated doors (incorporating passenger door control) and electro-pneumatic brakes. To work with the new cars many older ones had to be upgraded by converting doors to air operation and fitting electro-pneumatic brakes. All 151 motor cars of G and K classes and the 13 L and M motor cars were converted, after which they were called Q Converted stock; the G class became known as Q23, K class Q27, L class Q31 and M class Q35 stock. The new Q stock cars were known as Q38 stock – in each case the suffix represented the year those cars entered service. All the Q and Q Converted cars could work together, but not with F or H stock. The Q stock programme produced seventeen 8-car and twenty-seven 6-car trains of the usual 4+2(+2) formation as well as eight 4-car sets intended for (and briefly used on) the Met.

The self-contained F stock fleet was reformed at the same time into eleven 8-car trains (plus spares) now arranged into two 4-car sets, each containing one double-equipped motor, one single-equipped motor and two trailers. This work required conversion of the control trailers into motor cars, mainly by using equipment from former double-equipped motor cars.

The 1938 timetable required forty-seven 8-car trains and twenty-seven 6-car trains (and four 5-car trains as the District's contribution to the Circle Line). Off peak, many trains were just four cars; the widespread coupling and uncoupling operations were quite complex with three types of unmixable stock in use. Once the Q stock programme had been completed the new requirement was for thirty-seven 8-car and forty-seven 6-car trains. The formations just described were insufficient and the balance was to be made up using four 6-car and four 8-car trains of Metadyne-controlled P stock. The proposed use of District cars on the Metropolitan, and vice versa, complicated operations and increased training requirements and the reasoning is not obvious. However, a small number of P stock trains did find their way to the District for a few years, and some Q stock certainly operated on the Metropolitan until the beginning of the War.

The District Line was the unfortunate scene of a very serious collision that took place on 17th May 1938. At about 9.55am an eastbound Circle train had just pulled away from Charing Cross and collided heavily with a Ealing–Barking train that had come to a stand with its rear about 600ft ahead of the platform. The Barking train, which was quite well loaded, was seriously damaged and the rear car was forced into the car in front, mounting the underframe and destroying about 15ft of the 1905 wooden bodywork. Six passengers died and 43 were injured, in addition to two staff. Like most accidents there was more than one cause, the main reasons being an error made while rewiring a signal circuit the previous night, and poor handling of matters once the symptoms had become evident.

When the Second World War broke out in September 1939 it was inevitable that the District Line would be badly affected as its tracks ran on the surface – or just beneath – and the route through the City and the industrial areas of East London made it an

Q stock trailer 013176 freshly into service at Earl's Court in May 1939. What looks like a cab door at the left hand end is sealed shut and, inside the car, seats are provided in the space. Many trailers were later converted to motor cars when this arrangement was converted into a driving cab. The dummy cab end of 013167 was destroyed in an air raid at Plaistow in September 1940. The undamaged end was salvaged to repair Metropolitan Line motor car 14233 which had lost the corresponding trailing end in an air raid. LT Museum

The damage at Turnham Green was typical of bomb blast incurred all over the system. The signals on the left appear to be temporary work required by the wrecked gantry on which semaphore arms would have been in place. The view, taken on 23rd October 1940, looks west, despite showing Charing Cross on rear of car – this destination was in use the previous Sunday when the High Explosive bomb hit. LT Museum

unfortunate casualty of London bombing. In addition the District ran close to (and below) river level, so flooding was a particular worry – even a small breach of the Thames, or in one of the many feeder rivers that crossed the District, would cause widespread flooding and risk water getting into the tube network as well. The solution was to build several massive floodgates, one at South Kensington and one either end of Charing Cross. These comprised huge power-operated steel gates mounted in the tunnel roof that could be swung down to lock against a steel frame built into the tunnel, thus forming a watertight seal. The lower sill was designed to accommodate the running rails and small wedges were used to seal the flange-ways. By this means any inrush of water could be confined to a relatively small section of line. No gate was required east of Mansion House as the tunnels quickly rose to a level higher than river level. Signalling was interlocked with the gates and it was possible to run a limited train service when gates were closed as a precaution during air raids, the gates opening and closing for the passage of each train.

Early in the Battle of Britain, on the night of 7th September 1940, heavy bombing in the East End caused damage at West Ham and near Campbell Road and major damage at Plaistow where a train was hit, causing considerable destruction. The bombing continued for days and on 9th September destruction rained down upon Monument, Aldgate East, Bow Road and Parsons Green. And so it went on, repair gangs being constantly at work and the railway generally being patched up within hours. Some bombing caused much longer shutdowns. Parsons Green to Earl's Court shut for a week, Charing Cross to Mansion House two weeks (with a later one-week closure) and St James's Park to Sloane Square three weeks; but these exclude the sheer volume of interruptions of up to a day or two and individual station closures of longer duration. Several sites were hit more than once, such as Whitechapel, which was very badly damaged.

An LMS Earl's Court – Willesden Junction service train at Earl's Court before the Second World War.

Sloane Square ticket hall had been entirely reconstructed in the early days of the war, with up escalators linking each platform to the ticket hall from 27th March 1940. On 12th November 1940 the station building, ticket hall, staff canteen and new escalators were demolished by a 1,500kg high explosive bomb, the wreckage falling onto the last coach of a departing train and destroying it. In all, 42 people were killed. The entire section of railway was closed for 12 days and a temporary station came into service from 2nd December.

Later in the War the V weapons began to cause new damage and further service disruption, and by 1945 the Underground was heavily patched up. The whole system suffered from heavily reduced maintenance caused by loss of staff to war effort, diversion of resources to cope with air raid damage, and difficulty in getting components and supplies; in a sense this began the maintenance backlog which lasted many years. To try and protect stations from blast outside, many had blast walls built just beyond station entrances which did nothing for their appearance, but these were removed quickly after hostilities finished. In addition large signs were removed as a potential aid to enemy aircraft and lighting was reduced to support blackout requirements. Trains were blacked out by a combination of window netting, fixed to protect against glass splinters, and severely reduced lighting during air raids.

Following the bombing of the West London Line in 1940 the LMS Earl's Court–Willesden electric service and the Met's service to Addison Road were 'suspended'. Although track damage was repaired quite quickly, neither the LMS or LPTB were prepared to resume services, even after the War. It was evident the heavy traffic to the exhibition halls at Olympia could not be satisfied by road transport alone and the LPTB arranged to operate a limited shuttle service between Addison Road and High Street Kensington or Earl's Court during these events. The first occasion this service ran was 12th December 1946 for parties of pre-booked schoolchildren visiting Bertram Mills' Circus, and Addison Road was renamed Kensington Olympia at the same time. Ordinary passenger services operated from the following day, and then whenever major events were held. No alterations were made to track or signalling and trains usually reversed at the south end of the down main platform (though they could use any electrified road or reverse north of the station). Traction current was supplied from Earl's Court as far as the Addison Gardens bridge.

The rolling stock position at the end of the war was most unsatisfactory. The hand-worked door stock was overdue for replacement and there had been wartime losses of more modern sub-surface cars; the LPTB considered about 200 new cars were urgently needed. The terrible effects of war meant that labour, materials and fuel restrictions would endure for years and the government was rationing capacity, so the LPTB was told that it would only be allowed to build 143 new cars.

The engineers decided to introduce new trains composed entirely of motor cars, each car having lower-powered motors than hitherto; this arrangement produced higher rates of acceleration (though with lower top speed which saved energy) and the large number of equipments meant that trains were less likely to create major delays if one set failed. Many of the motor cars would not be equipped with driving cabs, creating a new breed of car on the District called a non-driving motor car (or NDM).

During 1946 it was decided that the best option was to use the entire 143-car allocation for an updated version of the 1938 designs (known as R stock) together with conversion of 82 Q stock trailers; this would provide a service allocation of twenty-five 8-car trains, plus spares. By this time the decision had also been made not to run 4-car trains any more so that new trains could be formed of a 4-car unit (with cab only at west end) plus one or two 2-car units (each with a cab only at the east end). By this means only three driving cabs would be needed on an 8-car train, reducing cost and improving the spacing of passenger doors. The conversion of trailers to R stock motors would leave the line short of trailers, so as part of the programme some older motor cars would be converted to trailers, and the L, M and N trailers working with the H stock would be upgraded to work with Q stock motors and fitted with air doors and electro-pneumatic brakes (the L cars became Q31 and the others Q35 stock). The introduction of R stock would allow the F stock (now 99 cars) to be transferred to the Metropolitan Line, releasing P stock to be reformed into eighteen 5-car trains for use on the Circle Line.

**F stock train at Olympia in the late 1940s. Trains usually reversed at this end of the Down Main platform (until the dedicated bay road was later made available).**

R stock orders were split between Birmingham (89 cars) and Gloucester (54 cars), the latter also converting the Q stock trailers into motor cars. The work proceeded painfully slowly given the heavy restrictions on industry, and the first new car was not delivered until 10th November 1949; the first new train didn't enter service until 17th April 1950. To improve flexibility the proposed mix of R stock was altered before orders were finalised to produce 31 trains (19 x 8-car and 12 x 6-car, including spare stock) and one spare east end driving motor; this was sufficient for 27 service trains.

The new NDMs were designated R47 cars and the Q stock trailers converted to driving motors were known as R38 cars, so designating their nominal age. Each 2-car or 4-car set was (for the first time on the District) arranged as a discrete unit, the cars being semi-permanently coupled. At the west end of the 4-car unit a Ward coupler was provided to enable a train to couple mechanically to an older train in emergency. At the other end of each 4-car unit, and at each end of a 2-car unit, a Wedgelock fully automatic coupler was provided which made air and electrical connections as well as mechanical, greatly simplifying coupling and uncoupling (only 6-car trains operated off peak). The trains were equipped with low voltage auxiliary circuits fed from motor-generator sets and for the first time avoided carrying a power busline along the train – as all cars were motored it was felt not to matter if odd cars occasionally lost current over pointwork. Inside the cars fluorescent lighting was installed for the first time and at each driving cab, a back-illuminated destination blind was fitted instead of separate destination plates (though on some cars destination plates and non-stop indicators were fitted next to passenger doors). Structurally the R47 cars were very similar to the R38 design, with some slight rearrangement of door and window spacing to even out the distances between doorways.

Even while the R stock was being built it was obvious the remaining hand-door stock required elimination, but the government was not prepared to authorise the steel needed. Working with ICI, investigation into the use of aluminium construction of Underground trains was already in hand and would reduce steel requirement significantly; eventually, a satisfactory method of construction was identified using a mixture of aluminium sheet, pressings and castings to produce an entire car from aluminium alloy, including underframe, though not bogies. Based on an all-aluminium alloy formula, authority was forthcoming for a further 90 cars in 1949 (to be known as R49 stock). To balance requirements 84 of these cars were NDMs and six were new driving motor cars, supplemented by conversion of a further 43 Q38 trailers to become R38 driving motors. Further H stock scrapping allowed the remaining 13 L, M and N stock trailers to be converted to Q31/Q35 trailers together with all 22 Q31 and Q35 driving motor cars which were converted to trailers. The alterations produced a further sixteen 8-car trains (and one 6-car), inclusive of spares, equating to about 15 service trains and mopping up the extra car built in the initial R stock order. The R49 cars looked virtually identical to the R47 batch though the construction techniques differed somewhat. 'Not stopping' indicators were not fitted and at first the roofs were left unpainted.

Experiments revealed that the aluminium surface offered a reasonable presentation to the public and was easy to maintain; one R49 car was delivered unpainted and entered service on 12th June 1952 to gauge reaction. One outcome was to place an entirely 'unpainted' train in service; this was complicated because so few R49 driving motors were built and while the first unpainted car of this train entered service on 1st October 1952 it was impossible to launch the completely unpainted train until 19th January 1953; nor was it at all easy to keep it as an unpainted formation given the vagaries of stock availability and scheduled uncoupling.

Mixed train of Q stock at Bromley around 1953, heading west. The leading car is a Q23 and the very different profile of two Q38 cars may be seen.

With the arrival of the R stock it was possible to eliminate the handworked-door stock from normal service operation. The last C, D and E stock cars in general use were all disposed of in February 1954; twelve assorted cars remained for use on Olympia Exhibition services until February and March 1958 when modern trains (with air doors) were substituted.

The introduction of air doors made the operation of the side-fitted non-stop indicators and destination plates very awkward. Provided by a limited number of passenger doorways on each side of the train, staff at reversing points could easily alter those on the platform side. On hand door stock changing those on the offside required the guard merely to open the nearest door and lean out to change the plates or swivel the non-stop station indicators to correct position. When air doors were introduced there was no means of opening individual doors in this way, so the practice began of waiting for passengers to get off and then opening all the doors on the offside as well; the guard then walked along the train to attend to the indicators. This was not ideal and by about 1950 was regarded as no longer acceptable. From the R49 stock onwards no non-stop indicators were provided and those already in use were removed. Reliance was now placed entirely on the train indicators on the platforms to suggest where a train would stop, or not. Furthermore, non-stop indications on boards on the front of trains had not been used since the War, being replaced by a board that simply said "District", though these non-stop boards had never been very useful. The R stock had destination blinds and never announced "Non Stop" on the front of the train.

View of the unpainted R49 stock cars coupled to a red-painted unit, probably in 1953.

Interior of newly built R stock NDM car. The design continued to use inlaid wooded panels on surfaces except those at doorways which were painted. LT Museum

# A New Era

On 1st January 1948, many parts of Britain's transport system were nationalised and much of the inland passenger and freight business passed to a new British Transport Commission (BTC) which was organised into a number of executives responsible for day-to-day operation. Among these, the LPTB's organisation passed to the London Transport Executive (London Transport, or LT) and the main line railways passed to a Railway Executive (trading as British Railways, or BR); the latter was broken down into various geographical regions. It is convenient to refer to the District Line's owner as LT hereafter. The BTC was abolished from the beginning of 1963 from when LT and BR became separate nationalised industries.

One pre-war scheme was soon resurrected. Notting Hill Gate station building had been rebuilt in 1928 but was otherwise little altered since opening in 1868 and interchange with the Central Line (which had a station across the road) was poor. During the early 1950s it was decided that linking the two was now urgent. A new (joint) ticket hall was built partly below the high street and the site of the former surface buildings redeveloped; the new ticket hall and subway interchange between the Central and District lines came into use from 1st March 1959.

With mounting train service intensity during the early 1950s, the junction at South Kensington became a major constraint. The smooth running along the south side of the Circle was disrupted by Circle Line trains crossing to the Met side of the station and delaying District trains. Nor was the arrangement ideal for passengers; at Gloucester Road and South Kensington eastbound trains could depart from one of two non-adjacent platforms, which was very inconvenient.

This was not a new problem. Even before the War, building a flying junction on railway land west of Gloucester Road was considered, but this was too expensive given the benefits achieved. During the 1950s, LT developed a property scheme for this land which would see it rafted over to carry a new West London Air Terminal for British European Airways (in those days most people booked in at an in-town terminal and were conveyed to London Airport by dedicated coach). This required major rearrangement of the tracks in the Cromwell Road area and offered the opportunity to deal with the South Kensington problem at the same time.

The scheme shifted the flat crossing east of South Kensington to a point just west of Gloucester Road and included removal of the troublesome Cromwell Curve together with many of the sheds and sidings. The former eastbound District track became the westbound Circle Line and the former Met westbound track became the eastbound line for District non-stop trains. The existing westbound District track remained unchanged, but the eastbound Met track thenceforth carried eastbound District and Circle stopping trains. The old Metropolitan bay road at South Kensington was dispensed with and the trackbed filled in to produce one large island platform.

The phased scheme was announced in 1955 initially to provide temporary facilities for British European Airways that involved rafting over part only of the western side of the triangle. The work required phased removal of the many sidings so that deep piles could be sunk to carry the raft and its superstructure. Once the deck was in place five new sidings were installed beneath it, after which the sidings and structures on the east of the site were removed. The new sidings came into use on 31st March 1957, though two existing sidings on the extreme west of the site were also retained. At the same time, Cromwell Road signal box was closed for modernisation and replaced by a temporary cabin nearby that controlled the new sidings (called Triangle Sidings) as well as the signalling at High Street Kensington and Earl's Court East.

Further east, track rearrangement proceeded in stages, the first of which was on 18th June 1957 which saw some new signalling and the decommissioning at South Kensington of the central bay road and Metropolitan signal cabin. The actual track rearrangement came into use from 30th July when the direction of running of the two central roads between South Kensington and Gloucester Road was reversed and final signalling commissioned. At South Kensington the District signal box was closed and the new junction-work was controlled remotely from Cromwell Road.

Cromwell Road signal cabin had been reopened from 21st July; the 20-year-old push-pull frame had been removed and replaced by a pair of push button desks; the left hand desk controlled Earl's Court (West and East) and Triangle Sidings, the other controlling High Street Kensington, Gloucester Road and South Kensington. Triangle Sidings, South Kensington and Gloucester Road were each provided with a new facility called an Interlocking Machine Room (IMR) in which an air-operated lever frame controlled local signals and points under the control of the Cromwell Curve push-button desks, but the existing remote-controlled signal cabins were retained at the other three sites.

**This view shows a 6-car service train coupling up to a 2-car unit (ex sidings) in the eastbound platform at Parsons Green ready for the evening peak. Alighting passengers were allowed off before the trains coupled, then the doors on the whole train opened and closed to allow anyone else on before departure.**

The temporary airport terminal came into use in October 1957, after which there was a lull in development activity. A second phase of the works began in 1960 when the existing deck was considerably enlarged and work began on a permanent terminal building and new BEA headquarters.

The withdrawal of the Uxbridge–Barking service in 1940 was operationally expedient but failed to resolve the mounting overcrowding to Barking and beyond. Worse, it proved impossible to run more than 32 trains an hour along the LTSR section where signalling was inadequate, reversing points too few, communications poor and train control in the hands of main line staff who (it was said) did not understand how to operate an intensive electric service. Even the 32 hourly paths were often not fully used because of wartime degradation of the District's older rolling stock. This was a far cry from the 40 trains that the LPTB felt necessary.

In addition to introducing new trains, options considered after the war included reintroducing through Metropolitan 8-car trains (against operating department resistance), persuading the LMS to remove goods traffic over the local roads at certain times, and allowing the District Line controller to exert more influence over the Underground service east of Campbell Road. The conflicting moves at Barking gave rise to suggestions to install flyovers at each end of the station. In the longer term, London Transport wanted to see both complete segregation of tracks, so its own services would be free from interference, and electrification of the LTSR lines to enable them to take a higher share of the traffic, perhaps even carrying all traffic east of Dagenham. For several reasons nothing was done for a number of years. The peaking of traffic in 1948, the ordering of new R stock trains, the lack of resources to implement schemes and the imminent arrival of a new nationalised management, combined to realise total inaction. After 1948 priorities slowly turned to the possibility of LTSR electrification, which would for a while generate many of the important benefits sought.

A BTC departmental committee reported in 1950 that electrification of the LTSR line at 1,500V (using overhead lines) and introduction of coloured light signalling would be necessary. So far as the Underground services were concerned it was noted that 32 trains an hour were presently operated as far east as Barking, diminishing to 20 an hour to Dagenham and 15 to Upminster. The services were very overcrowded, although the arrival of the R stock was expected to allow more trains to be operated as 8-car sets. Nevertheless London Transport aspired to run 25 trains an hour to Dagenham and 20 to Upminster. Signalling was unreliable and LT wanted it replaced east of Barking (though only 18 years old) and additional signals to the west. Underground service reliability was reduced by steam passenger trains that shared sections of the local tracks, and by off-peak freight traffic, both of which it wanted removed. The construction of flyovers at Barking would see Tottenham & Hampstead freight and through passenger services carried over the LT lines and further flyovers would allow complete segregation of platforms at Barking while retaining good interchange; both of these would also reduce delays and improve capacity. At this stage it was envisaged that the Underground would have two eastbound platforms (and one westbound) at Barking, and reversing trains would proceed via sidings east of the station (which would also be used for stock stabling). As the BR proposals required the land used by the District's Little Ilford depot for its own use, LT suggested building a new depot at Upminster by extending the site of its existing sidings there. Upminster station would also be altered to remove conflicting movements. At this stage it was still envisaged that the local lines would remain under BR control but developing BR plans broadly accommodated LT's aspirations.

It was impossible to begin physical works until 1955, by which time the local lines were to be completely segregated from the 'through' lines with LT taking responsibility for their equipment and exclusive use. An early move was to transfer responsibility for electricity supply and distribution between Campbell Road and Upminster to LT control from Sunday 3rd July 1955, including cabling and current rails – the supply was still delivered to and controlled from Heathway.

The segregation work was enormous. The entire line from Campbell Road to Upminster had to be resignalled to LT standards on tracks it didn't own and without interruption to services. Innumerable flat junctions between the local and through lines had to be removed, together with many other connections to yards, and other BR lines. At East Ham the vast area within the triangular junction (with the Woodgrange Park line) was needed for a new Eastern Region electric depot requiring the local lines to be rerouted round the northern edge of the site and the Little Ilford depot (used by LT) to be closed (in 1956 it was supplying 130 cars for service). At Barking tracks needed re-arranging to provide cross-platform interchange at a station to be largely reconstructed. New sidings were needed east of Barking and a new depot on land east of Upminster, where works had also to disentangle the Romford–Upminster service from those tracks used by the District (a connection was installed east of the station connecting the Romford branch to the main line tracks, crossing the District on the level; this was removed in 1968).

The largest single engineering sites were those for Upminster depot, on which work began in 1956, and between Barking and Upton Park where a fan of sidings was laid out. The works were especially urgent because East Ham could not be closed until both Barking sidings and Upminster depot were opened, and the track works west of Barking (upon which the BR electrification hinged) could not begin until the LT depot had closed.

Both Barking sidings and Upminster depot came into full use on 1st December 1958, though Upminster had been partially commissioned on 15th September 1957. Upminster depot was about a quarter mile east of the station and large enough to accommodate 34 8-car trains; it included nine under-cover roads and a 2-road lifting shop. The floodlit external sidings could take two trains on each. Shunting was controlled by an operator in an elevated control tower, using power-operated points and with two-way communication with drivers and shunters using 'talk back' loudspeakers.

**The new depot at Upminster soon after completion.** LT Museum

The first timetable saw 25 trains start and finish service there (Upminster sidings had previously supplied ten trains). A new LT signal box and new signalling came into use at the same time, track segregation from the BR lines having already been completed.

Barking sidings were shoehorned between the east and westbound lines immediately west of Upton Park station and the works required major track alterations. As completed, there were nine new sidings (five were double-ended), though five came into use on 9th June 1957. The LT signalling was nowhere near ready and at first access to these sidings was controlled from Barking East (BR) signal box. At Barking, flyovers east and west of the station came into use on 8th November 1959, allowing District trains access to platform 5 with cross platform interchange to up LTSR trains; the new Tottenham & Hampstead flyover had already come into use in January, with immediate relief to the District services.

In the eastbound direction plans differed from those proposed in 1950 and a single eastbound platform and bay road were provided for LT use; the configuration required retention of a length of former westbound line so reversing trains could rejoin the District west of the new flyover. The arrangement was unusual as the eastbound track remained on its original formation through platform 2 but the platform itself was shifted to the south side of the line by widening the existing island at the east end; meanwhile the west end of the extended island retained its original (platform 3) face that served a foreshortened track now ending in buffers. By this means good interchange from through or reversing trains was provided with down LTSR services, while level interchange was also possible from reversing trains to eastbound Districts. The new platform 2 came into use on 10th October 1960 whereupon the former platform became disused and some of the space was used for offices and sheltering for the Gospel Oak–Barking service passengers using platform 1. From 2nd February 1964 a concession was made to passengers coming off that service and wishing to proceed to stations east of Barking by additionally opening the doors on the old platform to allow them to board. This enduring arrangement is slightly odd in that the old platform remains unnumbered and for much of its length is exceedingly narrow.

The works along the 12½-mile upgrading were completed during 1961 when the rebuilding of Barking station had been finished. LT assumed maintenance responsibility for the new signalling as it was introduced, but track maintenance was transferred in its entirety to LT control from 18th July 1960. Upminster and Barking received limited new BR electric services from November 1961 with full electric service from 18th June 1962. The electrification scheme used overhead line equipment but not the 1,500V dc system as first planned because reconsideration of electrification standards in the early 1950s concluded that 25kV alternating current was the better way forward, reduced to 6.25kV where clearance was tight.

The District's electricity distribution system was also enhanced during these works. Amongst other things Plaistow substation was entirely replaced by new plant and Upminster depot had its own substation. LT had distaste for buying its electricity from the grid and once it got control of the electrical supply network switched back to its own source of generation, this time from Greenwich via 8½ miles of new feeder cables, though the intake and control room remained Heathway.

Although the track, signalling and electricity supplies were now supplied and maintained by LT staff, the land and stations were still owned and operated by British Railways, who issued the tickets and collected the money; LT therefore acted as agents of the main line in maintaining the equipment and was paid to do it. From 1st January 1968 the land and stations (except Barking and Upminster, which were still served by main line trains) were formally transferred to LT who took over complete responsibility – it wasn't long before LT's familiar roundel symbols replaced the Eastern Region 'sausage' name boards, though many BR signs lasted for years. Nevertheless fares along the whole route to Upminster had to be co-ordinated and many tickets were available on either route from either Fenchurch Street or Tower Hill.

The District's terminal arrangements at Kensington Olympia were soon found unsatisfactory as main line passenger and freight traffic increased. The outcome was to divert the shuttles into the rarely-used south west bay platform with its own segregated connection with the District south of Earl's Court Junction (which would be removed). There was only just room for a single-track link, but two tracks were retained on LT land. The new arrangements came into use on 3rd March 1958, following which the main line tracks were de-electrified. A handworked crossover (removed in 1992) was installed between the single line and the main line, to allow materials to be delivered to Lillie Bridge by rail.

Even prior to the Second World War the District's signalling was much upgraded, and in the 1950s work continued to replace the surviving 1905 equipment and standardise the rest, though the original safety principles were retained.

On LT-owned territory, signals were entirely automatic except at junctions where signal boxes were retained (except as already noted) in their original locations. From about 1933 there were no new installations of electro-pneumatic semaphore signals and from that point onwards they were all superseded by coloured lights, the last semaphore being replaced in 1954, at Hanger Lane Junction. There were still mechanical semaphores on the Southern Region's Richmond and Wimbledon lines plus one in Ealing Common depot that survived until 1965.

There had been some consolidation. In February 1909 the relatively new cabin at Minories closed as it was near Aldgate East and staff could be saved by combining the two. This concept was repeated in 1925 when Hanger Lane Junction signal box was closed and control shifted to Ealing Common, where the old mechanical frame was replaced by a miniature lever frame. A 1937 scheme to update signalling in the Aldgate area was frustrated by the war, leaving two very old signal cabins to control the triangle. From 19th May 1946 a new cabin was commissioned over the north end of Aldgate platforms which controlled the whole area, allowing the awkwardly placed cabin at Aldgate East (still at the site of the old station) to be closed. There was nothing novel about combining boxes, but such an operation required large amounts of expensive cabling and was not repeated.

In July 1934 an experimental scheme was introduced to operate the signals ordinarily controlled by the rarely used West Kensington West signal box from West Kensington East. Its success directly led to the route control system introduced at Cromwell Road. In each case the interlocking was achieved electrically from locally situated relay rooms, actuated remotely from the master frames at the signal box using telephone style cabling and circuitry. After the war the preference was to achieve local interlocking via 'slave' frames controlled at first by the 'master' frame (as at Cromwell Road) and from 1953 by push button consoles (as at Ealing Broadway). From 1955 interlocking machines (purpose built 'slave' frames) became the norm and are now all but universal on the District.

On installations since 1960 signal boxes have been omitted altogether, and interlocking machines have been controlled by programme machines; these stored a whole day's timetable and signalling moves on a plastic roll. As trains moved through the area each programme machine set up the moves required for that train by sending electronic instructions to the relays controlling the air motors on the interlocking machine; once the train was out of the way the machine stepped forward to deal with the next train. The first installation on the District was at Parsons Green from 9th October 1960. Putney Bridge followed on 20th November 1960, and between 1962 and 1965 all signal boxes between West Kensington West and Ealing Common were replaced by programme machines and IMRs.

To supervise train movements and to re-route trains during out of course working a central 'regulating room' was built at Earl's Court. From 12th July 1965 this facility (always regarded as temporary) was replaced by a permanent control room built over Heap's circular ticket hall at the Warwick Road end of station; this was intended to accommodate the whole of the District and Piccadilly lines' signalling and control functions (never achieved on the District) but although spacious at the time is now regarded as much too small for today's requirements. In the District's central area, Tower Hill was equipped with programme machines from the introduction of the bay at the new station in 1967 and Mansion House was equipped during 1969. Charing Cross was equipped with an IMR and facilities to reverse trains automatically or from push buttons at Earl's Court. The only other signal cabin was at St James's Park, which was closed.

During the resignalling of Earl's Court the east siding was extended at the east end to make a junction with the eastbound line beyond the point where the High Street line diverged at the Cromwell Road bridge. From May 1966 it was then possible for a High Street train from platform 4 to depart at the same time as a City train from platform 3, considerably reducing the delays caused by having (in effect) to cross Putney–High Street trains on the level across the main District service. Unfortunately the introduction of programme machines encouraged track simplification and a crossover at the west end of the station was removed, confining trains from Putney to platform 3 (when

**The rotunda entrance to Earl's Court designed as part of Stanley Heaps's remodelling in 1937. The upper aluminium structure dates from the mid-1960s and houses a control room.** LT Museum

getting them into platform 4 when there is a slot is preferable). Various studies have been done to see if this can be improved upon; a promising option is to alter the flyover west of the station to bring Putney trains onto the north track and those from Ealing onto the adjacent line leading to platform 3, but it is not a cheap option as the tracks are (in effect) in tunnel since the exhibition buildings were put on top. Replacement of the crossover when signalling is updated will probably be the outcome.

The large cabin at Cromwell Road was closed after traffic on 13th May 1967 following a period during which control of the dependent sites passed to newly installed programme machines and, where necessary, new IMRs; this cabin was soon demolished to make way for a vast development occupying the air space between the Cromwell Road and Knaresborough Place bridges. The last cabin at the west end of the District was Ealing Broadway which succumbed from close of traffic on 11th May 1974, the programme machines there also controlling Hanger Lane junction as had the previous control desk from 1959. The existing and relatively new air-operated frame was retained. From this point the only signal cabins left were at Whitechapel, which even in 2006 retains a lever frame, and at Barking and Upminster. A much-modernised lever frame also remains at the former Metropolitan cabin at Edgware Road; having passed its diamond jubilee this is currently the oldest frame on the Underground.

To deal with the extremely intensive service necessary during the 1950s, LT developed 'speed controlled signalling' (a refinement of the multi-home signalling) which virtually produced what today might be called 'moving block'. Under this system up to six home signals were provided on the approach to (and partly within) platforms. These cleared progressively following a departing train and to improve headways further an approaching train was allowed to pass the first homes if speeds were proved to have been reduced below 25mph at the first signal and 20mph at the second. Beyond that point the departure of the preceding train would cause the remaining signals successively to clear without causing a need for further braking, but if there were a delay causing an approaching train to stop it was now very close to the platform and would save useful seconds in drawing fully in. With everything working as it should, it was perfectly possible to see a train entering a platform before the back end of the previous one had left it. Such provision was an extra maintenance liability and after services were progressively reduced the extra equipment was removed during the early 1970s and headways closer than two minutes are now regarded as inoperable.

Power supplies were also gradually upgraded. From 1930, where new equipment was needed, static transformers and mercury arc rectifiers were installed and very slowly a programme for replacement of rotary converters was begun. The last rotaries to be tackled were at Earl's Court and South Kensington during the late 1950s. The work was difficult; while the new equipment took up less space than the old, sufficient existing plant had to be retained to operate traffic while work was in hand. Nor were working substations conducive to building operations and staged works were often needed to clear space safely for new plant to be installed. Materials into and out of these two substations could also only be moved by rail, at night. The Underground's largest substation was at Charing Cross, itself entirely underground. Replacing the equipment in situ was thought impossible so an entirely new substation was erected just east of the existing station building. Once the old substation was decommissioned the equipment was cut up, leaving a huge empty cavern behind. All this work, which was completed by 1968, latterly using solid-state technology, was co-ordinated with the introduction of a new high-tension network, area substation control rooms, and the entire re-equipment of Lots Road power station.

This view of South Acton station was taken in February 1959, shortly before closure. The single car shuttle train may be seen approaching this compact station, and evidence of the former second track may be seen across the bridge. Colour-Rail

During the 1950s the desultory South Acton shuttle saw its already light traffic falling further and was failing to cover costs. In February 1959 it was announced the service would be withdrawn with last train operating on 28th February. The track was soon lifted and South Acton LT station demolished, together with embankment approach, which now sits under light industrial units. During 1964 LT wanted to get rid of the bridge over Bollo Lane but the police refused to allow the road to be closed. Perhaps owing to the job having been made more difficult, the part-dismantled bridge deck collapsed into the roadway, closing it for some days after all, during which it was cut up. The two special cars that had operated the branch were withdrawn and scrapped. During 1964, staff shortage produced modest service reductions and the rush hours only District service to Hounslow was withdrawn. The last train operated on 9th October 1964, leaving that branch entirely in the hands of the Piccadilly. The District Line structure gauge has been retained as far as Hounslow Central on what has since become the Heathrow branch.

In the late 1950s, the need arose to scrap the last 12 H stock cars (used on the Olympia shuttles), to improve services to Upminster, and to increase Circle trains to six cars. This was partly achieved by building a dedicated fleet of trains for the Metropolitan modernisation (releasing P stock for District and Circle use) but there was still an overall shortfall. This was made good by purchasing a further 13 cars of R stock (this time designated R59) and converting a further seven Q38 trailers into R stock driving motors which produced one 8-car and two additional 6-car trains to augment existing services. This time new cars, which entered service in autumn 1959, were unpainted aluminium, while the R38 motor cars were painted with aluminium paint to match. This was not the first use of this paint; it had already been tried in 1956 on one car and later extended to sufficient other cars to produce what appeared to be a second 'unpainted' train – from 1962 all R stock was painted 'silver' as it came up for overhaul. Eight hand-door cars were scrapped during 1961 and the last four retained for departmental use.

A slightly odd District train service that ran along the north side of the Circle now needs describing. There were occasions when traffic along the north side of the Circle was busier than usual and rather than augment Hammersmith & City (or Circle) services it was convenient to extend the District's Edgware Road reversers to Aldgate, Liverpool Street or Moorgate; the Parsons Green crews which usually crewed these trains were trained for Circle duties anyway. This special service typically operated during the midday and early evening periods on Bank Holiday Mondays and the prior Friday (or Thursday at Easter, and occasionally Christmas Eve). The service seems to have got off to a tentative start for Whitsun 1943 but became more regular from 1945; a typical example is the 1949 Easter timetable, which showed the Thursday service operating between Wimbledon and Aldgate and the Monday service Putney Bridge and Aldgate, but in later years the eastern termini often changed. The holiday extensions stopped after 1964 but the pattern was resurrected as a regular Saturday midday and evening variation from 19th October 1968 until 5th February 1972. To add to the peculiarity of these services they appeared in no public timetables, the trains rarely had correct destination plates, and the services generally defeated the platform indicators, many of which were not equipped to show the required destinations. Nevertheless regular users seemed to know what was going on.

As previously mentioned, operating conditions east of the Aldgate triangle meant that the full central area District service had to be thinned out by reversing some trains at Mansion House in rush hours; in 1962 at least four trains had to be turned during the peak (the trunk service was then 36 trains an hour). The reversing movements themselves were disruptive and contributed to overcrowding at City stations to the east. Meanwhile Tower Hill station had become seriously deficient, had short platforms and was heavily overcrowded, especially by traffic interchanging with Fenchurch Street. Proposed redevelopment of the area also threatened to overwhelm facilities.

The outcome was to build an entirely new station a little to the east, and provide it with a reversing platform to allow most of the Mansion House trains to be extended as far east as practicable (even with today's more modest service some peak trains have still to be turned at Tower Hill). The decision was influenced by the existence of the old 'Tower' station site underneath Trinity Square where the old platform site could be incorporated into the new plans at modest cost. The case for sending the trains further east was examined, but was not felt possible without building a flyunder at Minories Junction, at prohibitive expense.

The first move was made in November 1959 when space for a booking hall was reserved in the ground floor of new offices planned for the east side of Trinity Square; this was occupied by LT in March 1960 and sublet on a temporary basis. Parliamentary powers were obtained during 1961 but work could not begin until 1964, with the new station replacing the old on 5th February 1967. At this stage only the eastbound platform was complete and westbound trains called at a temporary platform alongside the existing westbound line. Before reversing facilities could be introduced the westbound platform at the old station had to be demolished to allow room for the junction work to be installed, after which the westbound line was diverted onto a new alignment from 3rd September and the new westbound platform opened. The former temporary westbound platform – to become the bay road – was then completed, and from 22nd January 1968 most of the Mansion House reversers were extended to Tower Hill. With little reversing anticipated at Mansion House the bay road on the north side of the station was taken out of use in February 1968 and removed, just leaving the centre bay.

**A view of the tracks below the Victoria Embankment during works to replace the roof of the section near Waterloo Bridge in 1969.** Neil Davenport

89

The works at Tower Hill were part of a long-standing programme of station improvements designed to improve flow and lengthen platforms enabling them to accommodate 8-car trains fully. While the old catwalks did work after a fashion they were regarded increasingly as dangerous (particularly by H.M. Railway Inspectorate) and required extra station staff while 8-car trains were operating to ensure they were clear of passengers when a train started.

Platform lengthening was usually carried out during other works, and by the end of the war most had been lengthened although some awkward sites remained. A programme began in 1955 to improve the position, starting at Monument. The required 70ft extension was only practicable at the east end, but fortunately serious wartime damage facilitated progress. A bombsite over the tunnel on corner of Eastcheap and Pudding Lane, previously occupied by Lloyds Bank, was utilised prior to its rebuilding and occupation of the strong room was necessary.

Blackfriars was next; this time lengthened by 74ft at the west end. This site was awkward as it crossed the Fleet Sewer that had challenged original construction and ran under the roadway at the end of Blackfriars Bridge into the questionable made-up ground of the Embankment. The work was completed in March 1962 and comprised a new concrete covered way supported by massive beams resting on new concrete piers.

Westminster followed immediately, the works being undertaken between September 1962 and April 1964. The extension was only possible at the east end and was complicated by running directly under the Norman Shaw building of what was then Scotland Yard, the world's most famous police headquarters (there had once been a direct access into the building from platform level). It was necessary to make elaborate arrangements to support the building while the new structures were put into place, and the new extensions snaked past (and partly into) a particularly sensitive storage vault. When finished, the platforms were extended, one by 79ft and the other by 87ft.

Cannon Street had not been altered much since opening and had platforms that were slightly staggered with respect to each other. It was decided to lengthen each platform by 68ft, the westbound at the west end and the eastbound at the east end, thereby correcting the stagger. However an emerging property development scheme to build new offices over the main line station and forecourt (under which the District station sat), coupled with a road widening scheme for which the District entrance was in the way, meant that complete reconstruction of the ticket hall and modernisation of the station could be co-ordinated. The works were immense and included a new station roof and supporting structures, as well as a new ticket hall. The platform lengthening activity began during 1968 in the case of the westbound platform and 1971 for the eastbound; station reconstruction was in hand during 1970, the civil engineering work completing in 1972 and architectural finishes in 1973.

The conditions at Ealing Broadway were not regarded as very satisfactory. The District station was independent of the main line station (which for reasons of history also accommodated the Central Line). There was a bridge connecting all platforms half way along but ticket offices were all separate and interchange was inconvenient. In the early 1960s the decision was made to combine the stations and build a ticket hall serving all services on the site of the main line station. The new BR station opened on 28th November 1966, selling tickets for all services, and the District ticket hall closed at the same time; the station building in Haven Green survives but is now occupied by shops. Today, a bridge at the west end of the station connects all platforms both with each other and with the ticket hall, but there was a lengthy period before the District platforms were properly connected to it and for a while the only way to get to platform 9 was via the walkway behind the buffers. During this time, one of the Central Line platforms was shortened to allow level connection to be made between the District platforms and the steps to the ticket hall at the end of the Central Line 'island'; today this level access also connects with the up local main line platform.

The District's so-called non-stop trains were finally withdrawn from the October 1964 timetable revision, proving of theoretical advantage only. An immediate consequence was the disuse of the eastbound fast line between Gloucester Road and South Kensington, though it was not physically decommissioned until January 1966.

At South Kensington the very wide island platform allowed new steps down from the ticket hall to replace the narrow pairs that had been inherited from the days when there was a bay road. This having been done, the eastbound line was slewed across to the refurbished island to run alongside the north face, leaving the old eastbound platform intact, but trackless and with canopy removed. The new platform face came into use from 8th January 1967.

From 30th March 1969 all westbound trains were diverted alongside the southern side of the island platform and new points inserted in the tunnel to the west to separate the District and Circle services. This left South Kensington with just two platforms (it once had seven). The old south side island was then demolished (the siding and bay road had already been removed) allowing a huge concrete box to be built at the west end, housing new escalators down to the Piccadilly Line from an enlarged District ticket hall. These escalators came into use on 20th January 1974 and replaced a temporary arrangement where Piccadilly Line passengers had to use the steps down to the District

**R stock train in white livery at Acton Lane, between Turnham Green and Gunnersbury around 1977. The space to the left of the train was for the goods loop allowing goods trains towards London to dive under the Piccadilly tracks; this was removed about a decade previously.** Mike Horne

and new interchange steps half way down the island leading to low-level escalators that had come into service on 30th September 1973. Many facilities were left in a 'temporary' state in expectation of a planned property development scheme that (30 years later) has not yet materialised.

At Gloucester Road it was decided to widen the rather narrow island platform so that it reached across to the remaining eastbound line and could be used in substitution for the platform against the north wall. The new arrangement came into use on 1st March 1970 and required modifications to the canopy which otherwise would not have reached across the new width. This also had the effect of allowing the platform to be somewhat lengthened, though there was not much that could be done with the westbound platform against the south wall.

During the 1960s it became clear that the ageing Q stock would soon require replacement and the question arose as to how best this could be achieved. Eventually the decision was made to replace it by the CO/CP trains then operating on the Hammersmith & City and Circle Line (the 'C' prefixed the former O/P classification when the Metadyne control equipment was replaced in the late 1950s); these trains looked similar to the R stock. In turn new trains of an entirely new design were ordered in May 1968 comprising 212 new cars of what became known as 'C69' stock, enough for 35 trains and one spare 2-car unit.

As the C69 stock was introduced on the Hammersmith & City and Circle services, the existing Hammersmith & City stock was shifted to the District and an equivalent number of Q stock cars scrapped. The last Q stock train ran on the District on 30th June 1971, though some trains lingered on the East London Line. At the completion of the transfer some 270 CO/CP cars were available for service on the District, sharing about half the duties with R stock.

**A train of C69 stock at Whitechapel. Delivered for the Hammersmith & City and Circle lines, it became intermixed with virtually identical C77 stock when that was delivered for the District.** Capital Transport

# Recent Times

In 1970 most of the London Transport organisation was transferred to the Greater London Council (GLC – formed in 1965), where it stayed until 1984 whence it returned to government control prior to abolition of the GLC. In 1985 the Underground assets and operations were established as a limited company (London Underground Limited, or LUL), reporting to the parent body, now renamed London Regional Transport (but still called London Transport for short). Under local authority control considerable capital grants were eventually made to LT to begin the long delayed process of system modernisation.

By the 1970s many factors conspired to change the practice of 8-car train operation. The elimination of the remaining short platforms in the central area was incomplete and the remaining ones were problematic. In addition the constant coupling and uncoupling of units to produce 8-car trains in the peaks required ever-more-scarce staff and was increasingly regarded as an operational liability. In addition, passengers could not always anticipate how long an approaching train was going to be (6- or 8-cars) and that caused delays while they sorted themselves out. The decision was taken to standardise District train lengths at 7 cars, except the Putney–Edgware Road service which was stuck with 6-car trains.

This conversion, which began in 1971, was complex. The R stock formation was inflexible with each car being in some way different from the next. The solution was to shorten some of the 8-car trains to 7 cars by removing what was termed a No 2 car, which was easiest. The best of these was then inserted in the 4-car portion of the remaining 6-car trains, lengthening them to 7 cars. A number of No 2 cars were left over and scrapped. The CO/CP stock was adapted by removing trailers from several units and assembling 7-car trains from one 3-car and two 2-car units. There were sufficient 3-car units to maintain 6-car trains on the Edgware Road service. The operation of 5-car trains was not unknown. They were often seen on Sundays as the District still operated two Circle Line trains in each direction that day to maintain crew knowledge; it was easy to remove two cars (7-car trains were too long) rather than try and marshal 6-car trains every time. About this time it was found the silver paint being used on the R stock cars was not reacting well to the cleaning regime and future painting used white paint (previously unpainted cars were also painted white to match).

In 1977 the decision was made to begin replacing the CO/CP stock. Looking to the future it appeared the trains on the Edgware Road service were always going to be shorter than those on the main portion of the District. It was convenient to replace these first by buying a second batch of C stock, as 6-car trains of that type would fit the platforms. In consequence 11 further C stock trains were ordered (termed C77 stock); these were interchangeable with the earlier C69 cars and were to be maintained at Hammersmith (H&C) depot. The first C stock trains began operating on the Edgware Road service from 17th April 1978. The District C stock allocation meant that on Sundays they could operate the four District-crewed trains that operated on the Circle Line, keeping crews familiar with the route. This slightly idiosyncratic operation continued until May 1990 when it fell victim to a line-based management structure for which this extra complication was unwelcome; after a century of such operation, District crews are no longer trained for duties along the northern part of the Circle.

When the question arose about replacing the main District Line fleet there was no enthusiasm for increasing the length of trains. The only issue was whether to retain 7-car operation or whether to employ a longer car body such that six new cars would have approximately the same capacity as seven conventional ones. In the end the case was made for employing longer cars. A controversial issue related to door layouts where there was a strong body of opinion that by using a wider single leaf door, and by installing four doors per car side, the same boarding/alighting time could be achieved for vastly fewer door mechanisms (door failures were a major source of difficulty so the opportunity to mitigate the problem was welcome). There was a contrary view that the overall smaller doorways would badly impede flow and increase dwell times. Nevertheless, single leaf option was adopted, together with reintroduction of passenger door control which was intended to be compulsory at all stations.

The 75 new trains were designated D stock and were built (like the C stock) by Metro-Cammell in Birmingham. The cars were designed to be 18 metres long, compared with 50ft (16 metres) of a conventional car. Sixty-five trains were composed of 6-cars with a driving motor at each, a trailer next to each driving motor, and two uncoupling non-driving motors in the centre, either side of a wedglock coupler that would enable the train to split into two 3-car units. Ten trains had driving motors in the central positions, producing a float of double-ended 3-car units that could substitute for either of the single-ended units, maximising flexibility for maintenance.

**The D stock that began its working life in 1980 was the last pre-1992 Underground stock to be refurbished. The main programme began in 2005.** Kim Rennie

At first the D stock trains were operated with both a driver and guard but the design always allowed for operation by driver only and driver-only operation was introduced from 4th November 1985 (Circle trains had been converted on 22nd October 1984). When delivered, the stock was intended to be ventilated only by fans, but this was soon found quite insufficient in summer, and some relief was given by cutting out the passenger door control in summer to allow trains to ventilate at stations. This was hardly satisfactory and trains were soon returned to the manufacturers so that a number of opening windows could be fitted (in the end passenger door control was soon abandoned for other reasons, mainly the delaying effect caused by the need to operate the push buttons).

Probably the project causing the most change to the public's perception of the District was the huge amount of work undertaken from the end of 1986 to install the new systemwide Underground Ticketing System (UTS), involving computerised ticket issuing with encoded tickets which could be read electronically. A key by-product of this was the universal provision of new high-security ticket offices equipped with windows for manual service and prominent passenger operated ticket machines that could be serviced from within the ticket office area. At first the only stations to be equipped with automatic ticket gates to check all tickets on entry to and exit from the system were installed in central London. At outer stations (all those outside Zone 1) manual checking continued, the concept being that tickets would be checked on a random basis with penalty fares charged if passengers were caught without a valid travel document. During the mid 1990s gating was extended to all stations on the Underground, including Barking, Upminster and Richmond line stations which were still operated by British Rail.

Following many years of low investment, District stations had a distinctly tired appearance by the late 1970s and over the next 20 years many were refurbished. The largest works were at Monument (in conjunction with the Docklands Light Railway extension to Bank), West Ham and Westminster (in conjunction with Jubilee Line extension works) and Mansion House. At the latter station major refurbishment was possible in conjunction with a property development scheme which was built over the open-air platforms and required station closure for 18 months from the end of October 1989. Various other temporary closures have followed, allowing major reconstruction of stations and platforms deemed necessary after more than a century of punishing service. Where possible, works have been integrated with installation of small lifts to help the mobility-impaired. In some cases, such as Earl's Court, major reconstruction has proved possible with the station functional throughout.

Other stations that have seen major changes include Gloucester Road where a property development scheme was built across the platforms and provided the opportunity to build an entirely new ticket hall which integrated the previously separate Piccadilly Line station. The new station was substantially completed during 1992. The following year saw redevelopment at Hammersmith fructify; a huge property development scheme allowed the existing station to be completely rebuilt and a connecting bus station constructed, together with a new shopping centre. A model for efficient transport interchange, the site retained ticket halls at each end of the platforms. A slightly more controversial scheme was at Fulham Broadway where the station was largely covered over by a shopping complex and a new ticket hall built within it; the former grade 2 listed station building (dating back to District electrification) had to be retained but was adapted for use as a bar and restaurant. The new entrance was opened on 30th June 2003.

In 1988, the District Line was established as a distinct management unit within the Underground, having a large measure of day-to-day responsibility for service provision and in due course for most routine maintenance. This has since all changed again. With the establishment of a mayor and assembly for London, an executive arm was established in 2000 called 'Transport for London', to which London Underground Ltd was transferred from 15th July 2003. In addition, the infrastructure and rolling stock have been transferred to infrastructure companies established by a government Public-Private Partnership (PPP), that of the District (with other sub-surface lines) now being operated by Metronet SSL, which provides trains, track and other assets on a performance basis. Operating staff remain with LUL.

The most intensive service is now just 28 trains an hour, but this is still too much east of Tower Hill and a small number of trains are required to reverse there. Whitechapel, Mansion House and Putney Bridge are no longer used as a regular reversing point (and the latter is too short for D stock trains), and Plaistow is only used for Metropolitan trains. Off-peak services are scarcely less intense, but are more structured, with all Upminster trains running alternately to Richmond or Wimbledon, and the Ealing service served by trains from Tower Hill. Wimbledon is also served alternately by trains from Edgware Road. Each western branch receives a ten-minute service. Since April 1986 a regular service has operated every weekday between High Street Kensington and Kensington Olympia, replacing the Exhibitions-only service; this was extended to Sundays from 1996.

Having been in service for over 20 years the D stock was starting to look tired and the question arose about its refurbishment. In July 2002 a sample trailer car was refurbished to gauge reaction, though the whole unit was painted in corporate external livery. During 2004 trains began to be sent to Bombardier's works at Wakefield for refurbishment, the first being returned in November with all other trains gradually following on; they began to enter service from 2nd June 2005. Unfortunately it became necessary to replace all the D stock bogies before the refurbishment, and this programme necessarily began in 2000 following the discovery of cracks that would have been difficult to repair.

In 2004/5 the Underground carried its largest ever number of customers – over 3 million on each weekday – with nearly 560,000 of them using the District. This number is still rising and is putting great pressure on the infrastructure that requires extensive closures at weekends, to upgrade track and other facilities, though reliability improvement is already evident. In the longer term, PPP partner Metronet plans to introduce new trains from 2013 and the signalling and control systems from 2016 so the existing wide mix of equipment is going to have to last for many more years yet. Station refurbishment is already in hand though, and by 2011 some 15 District stations should have been entirely modernised and a further 33 refurbished. Among the larger works is busy Victoria, which has been wholly inadequate for the traffic using it for many years.

The District serves 60 stations and operates over 64km (40 miles) of track. It is one of the longest and most intensively used lines on the network – a far cry from its well-intentioned but financially disastrous beginnings.